To Terry & Pam,

With my very best wishes,

Mike

The Worst Golf Course Ever

Acknowledgements

First and foremost, I would like to thank the Cambridge University Golf Club and in particular the President, Professor Adrian Dixon, and the Senior Treasurer, Chris Blencowe for providing me with access to the CUGC minute books. Without that starting point, this book would not have got off the ground. They were also kind enough to read and provided comments on my drafts and I greatly appreciate their unflagging support and enthusiasm from start to finish.

Once again, I engaged Hart McLeod to convert my text and images into the final product. Many thanks to Graham for his diligent editing and to Jo and her team for their design work and efficient management of the production process.

Web searches save a lot of legwork these days but nevertheless I am grateful to have had access to a number of libraries and archives. On my doorstep, Cambridge University Library is a wonderful depository of so much historic material, including golf. I am grateful to Pat Aske, the Librarian at Pembroke College, Tang Yaye at the Cambridgeshire Archives, and the Cambridgeshire Collection at the Central Library. Further afield, thanks go to Angela Howe at the British Golf Museum, the Special Collections at the University of St Andrews and the Tyne & Wear Archives.

I received great support from a number of old Blues who cheerfully responded to my numerous queries. Thanks go to Charles Harrison, David Normoyle, Ian Pattinson, Dai Rowley-Jones, Donald Steel, Nigel Theyer and others.

I was extremely fortunate to have had the most generous support from the eminent golf historian, David Hamilton. Not only did he read through my entire manuscript and provide detailed comments and guidance, he also provided me with access to his many contacts to assist me with any queries that I was chasing. Thank you, David.

Lastly, I would like to thank my non-golfing wife, Charlotte. She must have thought that as I got older that my interest in golf might wane somewhat. She did not anticipate my growing enthusiasm for researching and writing about the subject. Given that, she is mostly patient with me and always supportive.

Contents

Foreword

Mike Morrison's account of *The Worst Golf Course Ever*, including the formation of the Cambridge University Golf Club with its first proper course on Coldham Common, is a fantastic read. I will not spoil the debate as to whether it should be called Coldham Common or Coldham's Common. That is for the reader to enjoy, along with the account of the marshy muddy course beset with obstacles such as a rifle range running through the middle of it! Mike has made full use of his PhD training in energy economics at Cambridge to undertake the research necessary for this masterly book, with many hours spent in the University and college libraries. It is only a pity that he did not do it as a mature student and thereby put himself in with a chance to be selected for the blues team at the advanced age of fifty-nine!

It is a serious piece of research, fully worthy of a historian and may render all future scholarly activity in this area redundant. Amongst other things, we discover how CUGC, from modest beginnings as one of the first golf clubs in England, became one of the largest by the 1890s; we hear of exhibition matches on Coldham Common involving Open Champions; and we gain an extraordinary insight into a rather eccentric individual, W T Linskill, who in 1878 got the first Varsity golf match up and running. It remains one of the oldest amateur fixtures in golf.

But that is not all. During his lengthy research on the topic, Mike discovered that some of CUGC's early trophies had gone missing. His detective work to identify their whereabouts and oversee their eventual recovery is a riveting story in its own right.

All golfers, historians of the Victorian era and members of CUGC and the Oxford and Cambridge Golfing Society will greatly enjoy this book. I am personally extremely proud that it has been published during the period while I had the privilege of holding the reins as President for a few years of its illustrious history. We are all enormously grateful to Mike for all his endeavours on our behalf.

Adrian K Dixon
Cambridge

Preface

Many golf courses, when their praises are sung, are said to be laid out on hallowed turf or to be hidden gems. Coldham Common[1] in nineteenth century Cambridge fell into neither category.

Bernard Darwin, the grandson of Charles, played golf there both as a child with his father Francis Darwin and as an undergraduate member of Cambridge University Golf Club (CUGC) in the mid-1890s. When his seminal work, *The Golf Courses of the British Isles*, was published in 1910 he wrote selectively about the best ones at that time. But he made one exception. And that one was Coldham Common which he famously described as 'the worst course I have ever seen, and many others would probably award it a like distinction'. But Coldham Common survived, and indeed thrived, for a quarter of a century. At its peak, hundreds of red-coated undergraduates were playing golf there, making it one of the largest golf clubs in the country. Despite the trying circumstances, it must have had something going for it. But what? It was from this intriguing starting point that I wanted to dig deeper to uncover the story of golf at Coldham Common.

When I wrote *The Links on the Hills*, a history of the Old Course at the Gog Magog Golf Club, I included a brief chapter on golf in Cambridge, covering the period prior to 1901, the year the Gogs was formed. That might have been that. However, when they heard about my research, the President and Senior Treasurer of CUGC, Professor Adrian Dixon and Chris Blencowe respectively, were kind enough to provide me with access to the club's historical records. These consisted of two very large tomes of (mostly) hand written minutes of the club's activities dating back to 1889. After a few visits to examine these, I felt convinced that there was an enriched story to tell about the golfing undergraduates at Cambridge in the nineteenth and early twentieth century.

This book concentrates on the first half century of CUGC's existence, from the late 1860s until the First World War brought golf to a halt. By then, a path had been taken (and a course chosen) and, by and large, it is the one that the club remains on to this day. It would be wrong to dismiss all that came after, but

---

[1] Today it is called Coldham's Common. In the past, it has sometimes been known as Coldham and at others Coldham's, sometimes both at the same time. In relation to the Cambridge University Golf Club during the Victorian era, it was almost always called Coldham Common, so I have retained that throughout when referring to the golf course.

crucial decisions made during this earlier era have created a lasting legacy. And here we are nearly one hundred and fifty years after the first golf ball was struck in Cambridge and CUGC is still going strong.

The material within relies on three primary sources of reportage. *The Field, The Country Gentlemen's Newspaper*, a national weekly sporting publication, is available at the Cambridge University Library on microfilm, dating back to the 1850s, although I drew on it mainly from the late 1860s to the mid-1890s. Reports of golf in Great Britain started out with occasional articles under the heading 'Pastimes', but by 1890 golf would have its own section and take up a page or two each Saturday. I rather tortuously wound my way through reels and reels of such articles specifically in search of those about golf in Cambridge. *The Cambridge Review, A Journal of University Life and Thought*, a student journal but also with material written by university staff, was first printed in 1879 and was available weekly within term time. Initially there were only a few reports about CUGC but by the mid-1890s this had grown to around thirty articles per academic year. Often these were similar to those that appeared in *The Field* but, importantly, not always.

The minutes of CUGC begin on 30 November 1889. Perhaps there were earlier ones, but if they still exist it is not known where they might be. Through the period of interest, they are hand-written by the honorary secretary of the day with occasional pasted-in clippings of match reports from newspapers. Although *Golf*, which commenced publication as a weekly in 1890, also contained articles about CUGC, these were essentially replicas of those that appeared in *The Field* or *The Cambridge Review*.

By far the most important chronicler of CUGC and its activities was William T Linskill. At the behest of his father, he reluctantly moved from St Andrews to Cambridge. He started writing to *The Field* in 1876 when he was twenty, even before he had been admitted as an undergraduate to Jesus College. He was to become the central figure in the development of golf at Cambridge over the next twenty years. He was a diligent and quite prolific reporter of the goings-on at Coldham Common. We are extremely lucky to have had him and his writings at all. But for fortuitous timing, he would have lost his life, when only age twenty-four, in one of the most catastrophic events of the Victorian era, the Tay Bridge disaster of 1879.

All of the articles in *The Field* about CUGC until the mid-1890s, and a few more besides, almost certainly come from Linskill's hand. The same is likely to be true for *The Cambridge Review* articles. Linskill was the honorary secretary of CUGC from 1887 until he left Cambridge for good to return to St Andrews in 1896.

Perhaps that is why the minute books that exist today begin at around the time of his tenure. His vast output of reports to the press, correspondence on golfing matters and the club's minutes, provide the basis for almost all that we now know about CUGC's activities from this era. Without him, there may have been little to write about today. Instead, we have detailed results of competitions and fixtures, occasional in-depth reports of important matches and, at least as interesting, his anecdotes, asides and general musings on the challenges of keeping golf going at Coldham Common.

In addition to Linskill, we are also fortunate that Bernard Darwin, the doyen of golf writers, was very familiar with 'the unspeakable mud' of Coldham Common. In his autobiographies and the numerous anthologies, put together from his articles he had published in *Country Life*, *The Evening Standard* and *The Times*, we find personal anecdotes of his time at Cambridge, sketches of the colourful characters involved in CUGC and, despite the trying nature of it, his nostalgic fondness for Coldham Common.

And so, we have a wealth of information at a level of detail that not many other golf clubs established during that era can call upon. The result is a revealing social history about these privileged young men playing golf in some of the least attractive circumstances ever.

Michael B Morrison

CAMBRIDGE UNIVERSITY
GOLF CLUB c. 1890

1

Introduction

Sport has always been an important aspect of the life of the undergraduate at Cambridge and sometimes not always legally. In 1574, the Vice-Chancellor of the University and Heads of Colleges issued a decree forbidding:

> *Scholars of what degree so ever, to resort or go to any play or game either kept at Gogmagog Hills or elsewhere within five miles of Cambridge on pain of a fine of 6s 8d.*[2]

There is some evidence that the ban referred to the playing of Olympic-style games, although this may also have included bull-baiting as well as pursuits of more Corinthian ideals.

It was during the Victorian era that sport really took off in England, both in terms of participation and spectating. Cambridge and Oxford were very much in the vanguard. The first sporting contest between the two universities was a cricket match played at Lord's on 4 June 1827. This was followed shortly after in 1829 with the first boat race. Varsity athletics started in 1864, the rugby match in 1872 and association football in 1873. Golf tentatively followed in their footsteps when, on 6 March 1878, two teams of four players met at Wimbledon Common and played the first Varsity match, which Oxford won convincingly. It is one of the oldest ongoing amateur fixtures in golf.[3]

But the story of golf at Cambridge does not start there. Nor is it solely about the annual Varsity match. It is not even one story. There are four stories told within. One is a saga, one takes the form of chronicles, the third is a biography and the fourth is a mystery. They do not fit into a straightforward linear narrative. They are interrelated and affect the telling of each other. In order to explain this, the key elements of each are outlined below.

---

[2]Cooper C H, *Annals of Cambridge*, Vol II, p321, Cambridge, 1842
[3]Perhaps the only older amateur fixture is the Lindsay Shield played for in matches between Leven, St Andrews and Carnoustie golf clubs which has its roots dating back to 1873.

Cambridge University Golf Club

If the foundation and evolution of the Cambridge University Golf Club could be described as 'a long story of heroic achievement', then by that definition alone it is a saga. This story begins in the late 1860s when golf as a game and the establishment of golf clubs south of the border was only just getting underway. At the time when the first tee shot was struck in Cambridge there were only half a dozen golf clubs in England. An embryonic university club was formed but it only survived for a short time. After a hiatus, and with new people involved, it was re-established in the mid-1870s at Coldham Common.

The club at first grew slowly in numbers, consisting of a mixture of undergraduates with a Scottish upbringing and absolute beginners keen to give the game a try. However by the late 1880s, by which time there were now around fifty clubs in England, CUGC experienced a dramatic increase in interest. Golf as a sport and a pastime became hugely popular in the 1890s – by 1892 the number of clubs in England and Wales had grown to nearly three hundred. The largest, and it could be argued, the most important at the time was Royal Liverpool at Hoylake, with a membership reported in *The Golfing Annual* approaching 700. Next in size came three clubs, all reported to have around 500 members each – St George's at Sandwich in Kent, Tooting Bec in London and, quite remarkably, Cambridge University at Coldham Common.

But these heady days for CUGC were not to last. Despite the fact that golf, by the turn of the century, had become ubiquitous, with over a thousand clubs in England alone, CUGC was in decline. The nub of it was the ever worsening conditions at Coldham Common and the emergence of better places to play golf in the surrounding area. Decisive action was needed. And, in a remarkably short period of time, CUGC obtained an outcome that has stood the test of time. Perhaps, until now, it was little understood how that actually came about.

Coldham Common

At the heart of this book is the story of golf at Coldham Common, a detailed chronological account covering the last quarter of the nineteenth century.

Cambridge is not obvious golfing country. It is flat, largely underlain with gravel and clay, and far inland from the coastal dunes where golf had traditionally been played. But in the mid-nineteenth century it had a number of green expanses designated as common land open to all, as it still does to this day. Early attempts were made to play on a number of these, but they did not last long for a variety of good reasons. The search for places to play even extended to Royston, a 15-mile train journey away. Finally, these pioneering golfers alighted upon Coldham's Common, about one hundred acres of land on what was then the outskirts of Cambridge, literally on the other side of the tracks.

It is well-recorded that the circumstances for golf at Coldham Common were bleak from the very start. The terrain was flat and featureless. Hazards consisted of a few foul-smelling drainage ditches; no bunkers were ever allowed to be created. It was usually muddy and often waterlogged. Golf was only permitted from October until mid-May each year as the cattle took precedence in the summer months. Most golf reports began with reference to biting winds blowing in from the Urals, torrential rain and sometimes snow and ice throughout the harsh winter months. But if golf was stopped at all it was due to the grass being too long in the Easter term just prior to the cows arriving. To make matters worse, the golfers had to share the space with the Volunteers who had an 800-yard long rifle range down the middle of the Common complete with butts for targets. When in use, it was a hazard to the golfers in the truest sense of the word.

Further challenges lay ahead: draining the common, proposed railway lines and managing the caddies, or as Bernard Darwin described them, 'hooligans in embryo'. Despite all of this, Coldham Common prospered. To accommodate the growing number of golfers, the course had to be extended from nine to eighteen holes in the late 1880s; and, in the early 1890s, an expensive new clubhouse was built, complete with a house for the professional and his family.

But it could not last. The problems at Coldham Common eventually became insurmountable. It is the classic tale of a rise followed by a fall, but how it lasted so long still beggars belief. But Coldham's demise did not mark the end of golf in Cambridge for undergraduates. A new course was built near Coton to the west of Cambridge. Little was previously known about this course, but now we have a clearer picture which includes, rather surprisingly, the role of some very well-known golfing figures.

The story of golf at Coldham Common and latterly at Coton followed the rhythms of the academic year with its three terms, Michaelmas, Lent and Easter (with typically less golf in the Easter term due to examinations and end-of-year social activities). Each October there was a sense of renewal at CUGC with men having gone down and fresh faces arriving. There were specific competitions held each term and in due course a regular pattern of matches played in anticipation of the climax to each year, the Varsity match. But within this general scheme of things, events occurred and important changes took place.

Within the book, the chronicles are arranged into four distinct epochs – the formative years at Coldham Common, from the mid-1870s until the late 1880s; from the late 1880s to the mid-1890s when the club was at its most vibrant; from then until 1902 when Coldham was finally abandoned; and from the opening of Coton in 1902 until the First World War brought golf, and much else, to a halt.

W T Linskill

The third story is a biographical account of the life and times of this rather curious Victorian gentleman – William Thomas Linskill – without whom there would be no book at all. Linskill is most often spoken of as the founding father of the Cambridge University Golf Club and as the key figure in the establishment of the annual Varsity golf match. But the story is more complex than that and so, in fact, was Linskill. Linskill, the beating heart of CUGC for over twenty years, was supremely eccentric. While he played golf most days, he also had an eclectic range of other interests. He was a larger than life character. If you had met him, you would not forget him.

Although he was an extremely diligent chronicler of the times, he could also be prone to partisanship and on occasions his reports could be somewhat self-centred. A more kindly critic you could not imagine than Bernard Darwin. But even he thought that at times Linskill held rather arbitrary views. So, this portrayal of him has a purpose – to develop a deeper understanding of who he was and what his motivations were so that we can better evaluate what he achieved and the legacy that he left behind.

The biography of Linskill has been split into three parts within the book – his family background, his two decades in Cambridge, and then his later years when he 'retired' to St Andrews. It might surprise the reader to hear that Linskill's name still resonates in St Andrews to this day, but not as the paterfamilias of the Cambridge University Golf Club, but as the author of a book about ghosts.

A tale of two trophies

The final story told within is about the search for lost treasure. Like all golf clubs, CUGC held competitions for its members, with cups and medals contested for throughout each golfing season. The results of these competitions were widely reported over the years and the winning of them was highly prized. In the course of researching this book, I identified a number of these, when they were played for and who had won them. When shown the trophies currently retained by CUGC, I was surprised to discover that none of the earliest cups, medals or mementos were amongst them. And so, as well as writing this book, a quest began to see if the missing silverware could be traced, if it still existed at all.

Two of the missing trophies are iconic. In rather different ways they are both hugely important in the annals of CUGC. The Linskill Cup, named after our eponymous hero, was the major scratch prize for one hundred years; it was first played for in 1877, making it one of the oldest golf trophies in England. It has had a number of quite famous winners over the years, including Bernard Darwin who treasured it and Henry Longhurst who contrived to lose it for a time. The Dunedin Cup is of a more recent vintage, having been donated by Lord Dunedin in the late 1920s. However, it harks back to even earlier times than the Linskill Cup. It is a highly distinctive trophy, but only from knowing the story behind it can the secret of its appearance be unlocked. For this reason, it is perhaps the most romantic of all.

Donning my metaphorical deerstalker, I set out to see if I could track down the two missing cups. Like all good mysteries there are twists and turns, cryptic clues, red herrings, and a few blind alleys. Fortunately, I was not alone; I was assisted along the way by a number of old Blues who were only too willing to help me with my enquiries. Whilst deduction and persistence played their part, luck also took centre stage in the culmination of events. It would spoil a good story to say any more at this stage, so I won't.

2

Golf begins at Cambridge

Early days of golf in England

Cambridge and Oxford were important in bringing a number of sports to the public's attention, in particular cricket, rugby, athletics and rowing. Varsity matches became major features of the British sporting calendar in the Victorian era and the Boat Race remains so to this day. The rules of football and rugby emerged largely from discussions and developments at the two universities.

But this was not the case with the game of golf as we know it today – it was emphatically a Scottish creation. There is evidence that it stretches back to the fifteenth century. Institutionally, golf took off in the mid-1700s with the formation of golf clubs and golfing societies primarily in the vicinity of Edinburgh and at St Andrews. By the mid-1800s there were around thirty clubs in Scotland stretching as far north as Aberdeen and to Prestwick on the Ayrshire coast in the west.

At the time of the first Open Championship at Prestwick in 1860, there were only two golf clubs in England. First, and foremost, there was Blackheath whose earliest formal records date back to 1766, but where golf may well have been played since 1608.[4] On a less significant level, Manchester (subsequently re-named Old Manchester) was established in 1818, initially on poor quality ground on Kersal Moor. But it seems to have been more of a dining club for Scotsmen in the area with a bit of golf on the side; it was small in number and only active in stops and starts throughout the nineteenth century.

If a date were to be selected for the beginnings of golf in England, by Englishmen, it would be April 1864, with the formation of what would become Royal North Devon at Northam on the first genuine links course in England, otherwise known as Westward Ho!

[4]Following the arrival in London of James VI of Scotland, having become James I of England and Ireland in 1603.

Westward Ho! literally got the ball rolling and, by the end of the 1860s, there were three more clubs in England: London Scottish at Wimbledon Common, Royal Liverpool at Hoylake and Alnmouth in Northumberland.

The first Cambridge golfers

SIR, Having had my croquet mallet recognised by a Cambridge rustic as "something for tapping beer," I was not surprised at a whispered "Look at they hockies!" as K and myself proceeded for the first time down Trinity Street with a few golf clubs and a hole-cutter under our arms. Arrived at Midsummer Common, a hole is cut near the end of Park Street; then, having teed our balls, we drive for the Lock house[5], near which another hole is cut. At this point the small boys who had followed us retire, I fancy disappointed at our not having laid our cleeks on each other's shins. Thence we skirt the river for about half a mile, and returning inland to our starting point we find that we have cut a course of eight holes, over ground which is equal to the Manchester links in the uncertainty of getting a good lie, or rather in the certainty of getting a bad lie.

Thus began the first report of golf in Cambridge. It took place on Midsummer Common.[6] The letter appeared in *The Field* dated 4 November 1869 under the pseudonym 'Light Iron'.

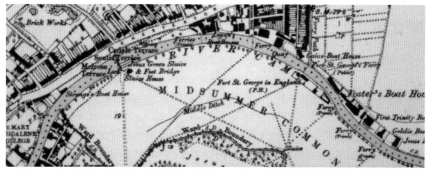

Midsummer Common in Cambridge, Ordnance Survey map 1886.

[5]The first golf hole in Cambridge would have measured about 280 yards.
[6]This part of the common, near Jesus College, was also known as Jesus Green. When Victoria Avenue was built in 1890, dissecting the common, Jesus Green and Midsummer Common became two separate areas as they are today.

The correspondent added that:

> *I don't suppose we played more than four or five games over this course during the Michaelmas term last year, and not so many in the Lent term following.*

So, this would imply that the course was laid out sometime between October and December 1868, only four years after Westward Ho! was established.

We have a fairly good idea who these two pioneering golfers were. The letter to *The Field* by 'Light Iron' referred to 'K' and later in the same article there is mention of Kellner being involved in a golf match at Royston. Cecil George Kellner was reading law at King's at the time. He was born in India in 1850. His father, Sir George Welsh Kellner, who was a British colonial administrator, was born in Calcutta. It is possible, therefore, that young Kellner learned his golf in Calcutta as it had been played there since a club was formed in 1829.

Earlier writers on the history of golf in Cambridge have suggested that, 'Light Iron', was one Andrew Graham Murray, a Trinity law student.[7] However in his authoritative work, *Social Links*, the author Donald Cameron concluded that 'Light Iron' was in fact George Gosset, a fellow student of Kellner's at King's.[8] Cameron uncovered another letter written to *The Field* in 1877 in which 'Light Iron' revealed himself to be 'a born and bred English golfer'. Gosset was from Devon while Graham Murray was a Scot.

George Gosset was born in 1847, the son of the Vicar of Northam in North Devon, the Rev. Isaac Henry Gosset. One of I H Gosset's sisters, Emily, had married George Moncrieff, an officer in the Royal Scots Fusiliers who was from St Andrews. Gosset learned to play golf on visits to his new brother-in-law and sister north of the border. Having taken to the game, he was involved in creating a rudimentary course at Northam Barrows in the 1850s. It was here that young George started learning to play golf in 1855, aged eight.

In 1860, at the behest of I H Gosset, Old Tom Morris came down from Prestwick (where he was the Keeper of the Green at the time) to visit Northam for a month to re-arrange the course. In 1864, the North Devon club was formed and Rev I H Gosset became its first captain.[9] A couple of years later, following school at Eton, the talented young golfer, George Gosset, went up to Cambridge, presumably taking his hickories, gutta percha balls and hole cutter with him.

---

[7]Browning R, *A History of Golf – The Royal and Ancient Game*, London, 1955
[8]Cameron D M, *Social Links – the Golf Boom in Victorian England*, Cambridge, 2010
[9]In 1867 HRH the Prince of Wales consented to it becoming a Royal golf club.

At this point, we need to bring the other golfing pioneer mentioned earlier into the picture, namely Andrew Graham Murray. He was born in Edinburgh in 1849, the son of a solicitor. He learned how to swing a golf club from a tutor at school in Perthshire, like Gosset, around the age of eight. But he only began to play golf at Musselburgh in 1866 during his holidays from school at Harrow. On his eighteenth birthday in 1867 he was elected as a member of the Honourable Company of Edinburgh Golfers.[10] He went up to Cambridge in 1868 although he thought that it was probably 1869 before he brought his clubs with him. It is also noted in his time at university that he was 'one of the first to ride a penny-farthing bicycle in the streets of Cambridge'.[11]

So, it was not long after Gosset and Kellner laid out their rudimentary course on Midsummer Common that Graham Murray started practising there too and soon he and Gosset would meet up and become friends on the strength of their common passion. They agreed that Midsummer Common was unsatisfactory as a place to play golf:

> *In the first place it was a place where you really could not have a links;*
> *secondly, you would get into frightful trouble for hitting people.*

So they decided to go prospecting for a new place to play.

Therfield Heath

Gosset and Graham Murray went to Therfield Heath, near Royston, about 15 miles south of Cambridge. Presumably someone had identified it as potentially good golfing ground, spotting it from the train while travelling between London and Cambridge.

Graham Murray takes up the story of that day in the May term of 1869:

> *Gosset and I went over to Royston one day accompanied by two bags of clubs*
> *and a hole-cutter which he had brought from Westward Ho! In Royston we*
> *picked up three little boys and went up to the heath. Surveying the land, we*
> *started and decided here should be the 18th hole, and the tee shall be here.*
> *We settled that the first hole should be a long one, and we looked with our eye*
> *and fixed the spot where the hole should be. We hit two full shots, and then we*

---

[10]At that time, the Honourable Company played at Musselburgh sharing the course with three other clubs. Due to overcrowding they eventually moved to Muirfield in 1891.
[11]Venn J A, *Alumni Cantabrigienses: A Biographical List of All Known Students, Graduates and Holders of Office at the University of Cambridge, from the Earliest Times to 1900*, Cambridge, 1953

played the approach shot. Then we cut the hole, and remember – the hole was not cut in the way of making an isosceles triangle of which the base was the line between our two balls; it was honestly kept where we said it would be, and we did the putting. We went through the 18 holes like that, and I really believe that it is probably a unique round of golf. Well, when we came back again we thought this will do.

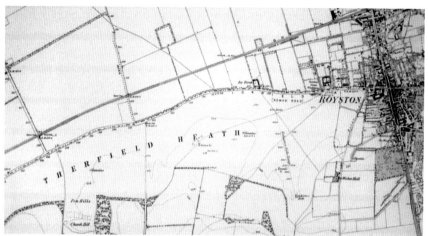

Therfield Heath near Royston, Ordnance Survey map, 1886.

Gosset, as 'Light Iron', wrote however that little golf was played during that May term 'there being so many other attractions, and only a few men having their clubs with them'.

To explore the possibility of starting a University golf club, Graham Murray and Gosset spoke to friends and they decided to put an advertisement in the local newspaper. One of the friends was Claude Cathcart Carnegie, like Graham Murray, a Trinity man. Carnegie was a Scot from Forfar who prior to arriving in Cambridge had spent a couple of years at university in St Andrews where presumably he had learned to play golf. In writing to Graham Murray many years later, he recalled that

> *..in response to an advertisement 17 of us turned up, including Gosset, you and myself. Gosset was elected Captain and I was appointed Honorary Secretary, and I took all the names and 2s/6d from everyone. So far as I remember, this was in 1869.*

So, and this is important, on the basis of this statement, we can conclude that a Cambridge University Golf Club was formally established with officers, members, a golf course and funds in the Michaelmas term of 1869. However, it was not a lasting success. Carnegie acknowledged that:

> *The end of term came soon after and next term I could not get them together again. Some went down; some said Royston was too far off, many never answered my letters, so it was left to only five or six faithful.*

There were reports of golf being played at Royston in *The Field*. In the edition dated 4 November 1869, it was noted that golf had taken place the previous Thursday, 28 October. Once again it was filed by Gosset, 'Light Iron':

> *A friendly contest was arranged between Trinity and King's. Mr Carnegie, one of the representatives of Trinity, was unable to put in an appearance; however, Mr Murray was willing to stand alone against Messrs Gosset and Kellner, who represented King's.*

It seems likely that the King's pair played as in foursomes, alternating shots with one ball, against Graham Murray playing his own ball. The match report followed:

> *The first hole was gained by Mr Murray, the next two by the King's men. The Trinity man won five of the next six, turning three up; and though the King's men twice reduced the lead to one, Trinity came at the finish, and won by four holes up, two to play. The byes were divided. Though a cold wind blew in the faces of the players going out, the play was by no means bad, Mr Murray being especially deadly with his irons. Mr Kellner drove some long balls, but was too much out of practice to play the short game well.*

One gets the impression that Gosset felt slightly let down by his partner on the day in question. Two other outings to Royston were reported during Michaelmas term 1869:

> *On Friday last Graham Murray, of Trinity, took a match from Carnegie by five holes, on the round of eighteen. On Saturday morning Kellner, of King's, beat Miller, of Jesus, by several holes; Gosset, of King's, beat Murray. The scores were Gosset 107; Murray 114; Kellner, 121; Miller far astern. The two King's men were to have had a match in the afternoon; but the rain which held up pretty well during the first round, came down hard, and drove the golfers back to Cambridge.*

Including Miller of Jesus College, this probably accounts for five of the 'five or six faithful' referred to by Carnegie in his recollection of the founding members of the club. Perhaps it is not surprising to learn that James Charles Miller was yet another Scot, born in Leith in 1848. He grew up at Manderston House in the Scottish borders which had been purchased by his father, Richard, in 1855.

The report concluded:

> *There will probably be a match between two Cantabs and two Members of the House of Commons early next term; and possibly a tourney may be arranged with the Blackheath Club for the May term.*

This seems to have been wishful thinking and no further reports appeared in *The Field* from this era.

The demise of the first club

With the lack of appetite amongst the student body to play golf on Therfield Heath, Gosset, the captain, and Carnegie, the hon sec, decided that it was not worth carrying on, and as Carnegie put it:

> *… all the result being the 2/6s … in my pocket.*

By 1871 this first flowering of the Cambridge University Golf Club came to a natural ending. Everyone associated with it had gone down and no new blood was there to take it forward. But what of the 'five faithful'?

Andrew Graham Murray went on to have a distinguished legal and political career. After obtaining his BA from Cambridge in 1872, he was called to the Scottish bar in 1874 and became a queen's counsel in 1891. In that same year, not only was he elected as the MP for Bute, he was also elected as the Captain of the R&A, where he had been a member since 1870. The pinnacle of his political career was becoming the Secretary for Scotland from 1903-05. He was raised to the peerage in 1905 becoming Lord Dunedin of Stanton in Perthshire and was a law lord through to the 1930s. In the 1920s, he captained Sunningdale four times and oversaw the legal aspects of the construction of the New Course there. In 1926, he was further honoured, becoming the 1st Viscount Dunedin. He died in 1942, aged 92.

George Gosset, after graduating from Cambridge in 1870, went to London to train as a doctor. He then practised in Abingdon near Oxford from 1876-83. He continued to play golf after Cambridge at Wimbledon, Hoylake and Westward Ho! with no little success. However, in 1883 he emigrated to New Zealand where he continued to practise medicine. Although golf took a back seat in his early years there, he picked it up again and became the New Zealand champion in 1895 at the age of 47. He died in 1931, aged 83, in England having only recently returned from New Zealand. If there was any need for further clarification of the position he held while at Cambridge, it is stated within the Register of Admissions to King's College (1797-1925) that George Gosset was 'Capt. C. U. Golf Club 1869-71'.

Claude Cathcart Carnegie did not graduate but entered the military and became a major in the 5th Brigade, Scottish Division of the Royal Artillery. With the death of his father, he became a Scottish Lord, of the Barony of Tarrie in Angus. He continued to play golf and was a member of the R&A. In his later years, he became a Justice of Peace first for Forfarshire and subsequently for Devon where he lived in Northam, playing golf at George Gosset's home course of Westward Ho!

Cecil George Kellner in his last year at Cambridge in 1871 became the President of the Cambridge Union Society. In 1872 he was called to the Bar but returned to Calcutta soon after. He died young, in Bengal in 1880, aged 30.

James Charles Miller married Maria Josephine Coen from Limerick in Ireland shortly after leaving Cambridge in 1871. He had two sons, born in 1875 and 1876, and in the mid-1890s the family home was in Kensington, London. Nothing more has been unearthed about him.

3

W T Linskill – background and boyhood

We now turn our attention to the key figure in this entire story. William Thomas Linskill was born into a landowning family in the northeast of England in 1855. He is often spoken of as the founder of golf at Cambridge and specifically of CUGC in 1875, the same year as golf began at Oxford. Furthermore, there seems little doubt that he was the driving force in getting the annual Varsity match up and running in 1878, one of the oldest and longest running amateur golf fixtures.

He remained involved with CUGC for two decades, as a golfer, the captain, committee man and subsequently as the honorary secretary before moving permanently to St Andrews in 1896. While there, he would go on to become a town councillor and hold the position of the dean of guild. He was the president of the St Andrews Antiquarian Society and specialised in collecting ghost stories about the 'auld grey toon' and giving tours to visitors on the subject. He died in 1929, aged 74, and is buried in St Andrews.

In this chapter, before he takes centre stage, we examine his family background, how he learned to play golf as a boy and how he came to be in Cambridge looking to play golf, a few years after the earlier golfers had all gone down.

The Linskill lineage

William Thomas Linskill came from a long line of William Linskills. The Linskills originated from Whitby in North Yorkshire. In the eighteenth century, Whitby was a major port. Great-grandfather William (1726-83), with other members of the Linskill family, was involved in the shipping business there. Through the wealth that this generated, he bought an estate and was lord of the manor of Great Moorsholm, about 15 miles inland from Whitby. Grandfather William (1766-1845) became a major landowner in North Shields and built Tynemouth Lodge there, set in a 40-acre estate around 1790. In 1806 he became the High

Sheriff of Northumberland.[12] He reached the rank of Colonel in the army and, to this day, there is a pub in North Shields called the Colonel Linskill.

Father William (1807-1901) was born in Tynemouth Lodge. He attended Harrow for schooling. In due course he entered the 28th Regiment of Foot and reached the position of Captain in the 5th Dragoon Guards. On leaving the army he took up civic duty and in 1849 was elected as the first mayor of the new borough of Tynemouth and was subsequently re-elected on two further occasions.

Captain Linskill married rather late in life in 1853, age 46, to Frances Arthur Charlotte Annesley, the second daughter of the 10th Viscount Valentia. On 25 June 1855, William Thomas Linskill was born at Tynemouth Lodge and would be the Linskills only child, as well as the last in the line of William Linskills.

The borough of Tynemouth was growing rapidly at that time and Captain Linskill decided to sell Tynemouth Lodge for development land in 1857. The Linskill name lives on in North Shields. There is a Linskill Terrace close to where Tynemouth Lodge used to be; in the 1930s, Linskill Secondary Modern School was opened (now closed); and today there exists a Linskill Centre, a thriving resource for the local community.

W T Linskill's father, Captain William Linskill, mayor of Tynemouth, c1850

The Linskills moved up the Northumberland coast to Warkworth where they purchased Morwick Hall, a late-Georgian house and estate in February 1857.[13] The estate apparently comprised of 740 acres for which they paid £25,700, a very substantial sum.[14] The Linskills were registered as living at Morwick in the 1861 Census, but they only remained there for one more year before selling the estate to Mr James Dand of Togston Hall.

[12]The High Sheriff is the sovereign's judicial representative in the county, while the Lord Lieutenant is the sovereign's personal representative.
[13]Morwick Hall was formerly a seat of the Greys of Northumberland (of Earl Grey tea fame).
[14]Fordyce T, *Historical Register of Remarkable Events*, Newcastle-upon-Tyne, 1866

Linskill learns golf

When Captain Linskill sold Morwick, when William would have been seven years old, they moved to Scotland, to Helensburgh about 20 miles north-west of Glasgow on the Firth of Clyde. There is no explanation as to why they moved there. Helensburgh in the mid-nineteenth century was a fashionable town with fine villas and mansions owned by wealthy Glasgow ship-owners and merchants so it was an attractive place to live. It probably had a richer social life than the rather isolated estate at Morwick. There was also a widely-known school there, Larchfield Academy, which Linskill attended, presumably as a day-boy rather than as a boarder. The Linskills were still in the Helensburgh area when the 1871 Census was taken, with William and Frances Linskill, together with fifteen-year-old William, listed as living at Glennderrie House.

It was presumably during their time in Helensburgh that the Linskills started taking summer holidays in St Andrews. In the mid-nineteenth century, St Andrews was becoming a fashionable holiday destination:

> *St Andrews was fortunate in having expansive beaches for sea bathing as well as ancient monuments and extensive cliffs and stone quarries. Sea-bathing had become fashionable among the health-conscious Victorians. Exploring ancient ruins, as well as chipping at rocks to uncover fossil remains, were pursuits for both gentlemen and ladies of a scientific frame of mind. St Andrews, with its resident community of intellectuals in the University and gentry in the Royal and Ancient Golf Club, became a choice summer resort for the increasingly socially aware middle classes from the heartlands of industry.*[15]

There is a curious family connection with St Andrews. One of the most famous paintings in golf is *The Golfers: A Grand Match played over the links of St Andrews* painted by Charles Lees in 1847. This depicts a foursomes match with over fifty figures watching it. One of the figures is noted to be Lord Viscount Valentia. This would have been the 10th Viscount Valentia, the Hon Francis Linskill's father and hence William T Linskill's grandfather. Viscount Valentia's estate was in Oxfordshire. No records have been uncovered of him being a member of the R&A or elsewhere and no reports of him playing golf have been found. He is believed to have been part of the Fife foxhunting set, so maybe his appearance in the famous golfing scene was merely via that association.

The story, as related by Linskill himself, was that he learned to play golf while holidaying with his parents in St Andrews at the age of 15, around 1870. He also

---

[15]Malcolm D, Crabtree P E, *Tom Morris of St Andrews: The Colossus of Golf*, Edinburgh, 2008

claimed on a number of occasions that he was taught how to play by Young Tom Morris, the son of Old Tom Morris who was the famous Keeper of the Green at St Andrews. Around that time, Young Tom was equally famous, having won the Open Championship four years in succession in 1868, 1869, 1870 and 1872 (there was no Championship in 1871). So Linskill, in all probability, learned his golf from playing with the then Open Champion, who was only 3-4 years his senior. In *The Field* on 4 June 1874, it was reported that:

> *On Wednesday, last week, Mr Linskill and Tom Morris, jun., played Messrs McDonald and Burgess over two rounds.*

One of the other members of this foursome, a boy of a similar age to Linskill, was Charles Blair Macdonald. He would go on to become one of the founding fathers of golf in America, and that country's first Amateur Champion in 1895. He verified that William T Linskill was one of his 'playmates' while he spent two years at university in St Andrews from 1872 to 1874.[16]

A St Andrews foursome, Scotland v America, consisting of W T Linskill and Tom Morris Jr against Charles B Macdonald and Edward R Burgess.

[16]Macdonald C B, *Scotland's Gift – Golf*, New York, 1928

Linskill kept scrapbooks throughout his life and in one of these, which is held in the British Golf Museum in St Andrews, there is a page titled 'A St Andrews Foursomes, Scotland v America', which includes photographs of the protagonists mentioned in the above match. The photograph of Young Tom Morris is a well-known one showing him wearing the Championship Belt which he won outright in 1870.

The Linskills must have liked St Andrews because they left Helensburgh and moved there. Later in life, Linskill wrote an article in a St Andrews newspaper in which he stated that he was educated at Larchfield and then at St Andrews before going to Cambridge. Presumably he was at one of the schools there or in private tuition to prepare for admission to university.

However, they did not stay in St Andrews for long. Linskill wrote on a number of occasions that he was in Cambridge in 1873. The move was clearly not of young William's choosing. He said that 'it was just something perfectly awful when I had to leave St Andrews and all my friends to go south to unknown Cambridge'. He further elaborated on this:

> *St Andrews meant golf and pleasure; the 'Varsity town in the Fens was compulsory. No two places in the wide world could be so absolutely different in climate, scenery, environment or social life. I shall never forget the shock I endured when my father resolved to give up his comfortable house in dear old St Andrews and migrate down to Cambridge. It was exactly like having all my teeth out at one sitting; it was a bombshell, an earthquake, and volcanic eruption all rolled into one, and it upset all my preconceived ideas about equity. I knew not the South in the least! But my stern, iron-willed parent never wavered for a moment, and to my utter consternation, off we went from St Andrews, lock, stock and barrel.*

You can almost hear the teenage William screaming, "It's so unfair!".

The worst aspect of the move to Cambridge was that there was no golf there. Later in life Linskill lamented:

> *After I left Northumberland when a child of only six years, I never saw England again until I was nineteen, and was taken very much against my will southward to Cambridge. What a shock I got! I can never forget it. The atmosphere and the intense monotonous flatness of the Fen country fairly paralysed me… but, far worst of all, no-one there had ever heard of golf! … I shall never forget my very first Cambridge party with my then tutor (how*

*many I have had!), famous old John Dunn of Shelford. When I spoke of golf
and St Andrews, the men and ladies present gaped and glared at me as though
I were a dodo or a harmless lunatic out on the loose.*

The above statement by Linskill, that he did not see England again until age
nineteen, would place him in Cambridge sometime between June 1874 and
June 1875. However, this must have been an error of recollection by him.
J G Harrod & Co.'s *Postal and Commercial Directory of Suffolk and Cambridgeshire*,
published in September 1873, gives Captain Linskill as resident at 3 Belvoir
Terrace, Cambridge.[17] Subsequent to this, we have an announcement in *The Field*
on 8 May 1875 that prior to the Spring Meeting at St Andrews, W T Linskill was
admitted to the Royal and Ancient golf club and his address was reported to be
3 Belvoir Terrace, Cambridge. Apparently his 'iron-willed' father organised this as
a birthday present.

Yet again, we have no explanation for the Linskills' re-location. Captain and the
Hon Frances Linskill would have been in their sixties by then. The only recurrent
theme would seem to be their son's education. Perhaps Cambridge was chosen
because there would be no golfing distractions? Once there he was enrolled
in private tuition to enable him to meet the necessary University admission
requirements.

Despite much digging, Captain Linskill and his wife Frances remain a closed
book as regards their lives in Cambridge. But, a folder of letters written by him to
acquaintances in Tynemouth has survived.[18] Three letters were sent by him from
St Andrews, respectively dated October 1873, August 1891 and August 1892. The
rest, dating from 1881 to 1898 were posted by Captain Linskill from 3 Belvoir
Terrace. In the 1881 Census it was noted that they had three servants living there,
all of Scottish birth. Captain Linskill died on 17 March 1901, living to the grand
old age of 94 and the Hon. Frances Linskill died on 14 May 1904, aged 89. They are
buried in Mill Road Cemetery in Cambridge.[19]

---

[17]Belvoir Terrace, close to the Trumpington Road in Cambridge consisted of five Georgian style
houses believed to have been constructed around 1825.
[18]File DX526, *William Linskill of North Shields*, Tyne and Wear Archives, Newcastle
[19]Their graves today (together with that of their grand-daughter May Seton Linskill) are hidden deep
in a clump of impenetrable bushes and shrubs. The couple's low profile in Cambridge continues, even
a century after their deaths.

Linskill in search of a links

Coe Fen

To re-cap, the earlier generation of Cambridge golfers had all gone down by June 1871. There was then a hiatus. Linskill had arrived in Cambridge in 1873 but not yet at the University.

In an article in *The Cambridge Review* (27 February 1896), Linskill provided a brief sketch of how he started playing golf in Cambridge:

> *It may interest players to know that golf was first begun in 1873 on Coe Fen, opposite the Botanic Gardens. There were three holes on this side of the Trumpington Road and four more on the narrow strip of grass over the other side of the road.*

The figure on page 29 shows a segment of Baker's map of Cambridge from 1830, which explains where Linskill's course was located.

It can be seen why Linskill first played golf here – it was right next to the family home in Belvoir Terrace, which is located just under a mile from the centre of Cambridge.[20] It is apparent that the three holes were on that part of Coe Fen beside Belvoir Terrace. The other four holes must therefore have been on 'the narrow strip' of Empty Common on the other side of the road.

The 1896 article also mentions an attempt to play golf on Sheep's Green (which was only about five minutes on foot from Belvoir Terrace) but it was too marshy. So Linskill decided to look further afield. The first article to be written by Linskill to appear in *The Field* was published on 15 January 1876:

> *Being a member of St Andrews club and a great lover of golf and while compelled to live in Cambridge the greater part of the year, it struck me at the beginning of last term to go on a voyage of discovery around the country and see if there was no ground suited to golf. I drove around the country on every*

---

[20]Baker's map does not show the Botanic Gardens on the opposite side of the Trumpington Road as they did not open until 1846.

side within easy distance of Cambridge, but found nothing the least to resemble links, on account of the flatness and marshiness of the ground. However, I have now found a small common in the Trumpington Road, about 300 or 400 yards long, but very narrow with some few small undulations in it. But beggars must not be choosers; and I have managed to make four holes and by playing zigzag a few good drives and iron pitches can be got, but putting is almost impossible except with a cleek, on account of the common being so cut up with horses feet. I have managed to instruct one or two friends in the game and we are now able to get us a tolerably good foursome. Is it not a pity that a regular club cannot be formed here, as it is (I believe) at the sister university? If good ground could be obtained, it would be certain to become a fashionable pastime.

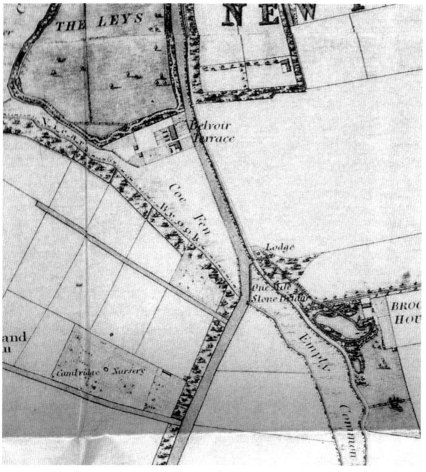

Coe Fen and Belvoir Terrace on Baker's map of Cambridge, 1830.

Linskill bemoans the fact that while he thought there was a golf club at Oxford, there was not one at Cambridge when he wrote his letter in January 1876. There emphatically was a University golf club at Oxford as its formation had been reported in *The Field*, taking place on 10 February 1875 in Mr D Campbell's rooms at Christchurch College. Shortly thereafter, a nine-hole course was laid out at the cricket grounds on Cowley Marsh.

More importantly, if no club at Cambridge had been formed when Linskill wrote his letter, it brings into question statements made by Linskill and repeated by others in subsequent years that the Cambridge University Golf Club was formed in 1875, as at Oxford.

Putting this to one side for the moment, the search for 'good ground' was underway. About a month after his first article in *The Field*, a second one appeared on 19 February 1876:

> *This game has now been started at Cambridge as well as Oxford. A suitable ground has been procured at Coldham's Common, and a course of nine holes laid out, which is two miles in length.*

Coldham's Common

'Suitable' the ground may have been from Linskill's perspective, but it was about as far removed as it could be from the traditional links land upon which golf was first played on the east coast of Scotland.

Coldham's Common is probably best described as transition land – the underlying chalk from the hills lying to the south merging into the watery fenlands to the north. It was created in the aftermath of the last Ice Age. As thawing conditions commenced, the permanently frozen ground melted turning the soil to slurry and releasing water which formed a pool. Sunlight would heat the water and further melt the permafrost making the pool bigger and bigger. It is thought that some 20,000 years ago, Coldham's Common was a muddy lake of melted sludge and slurry. Eventually, this leaked away into the ancient River Cam draining the lake and leaving a large flat-bottomed hollow.

Coldham Green or Common existed in 1300.[21] The derivation of the name is unknown. By 1700 it had been designated as a green common, allowing Cambridge commoners grazing rights for their cattle and horses.[22] Following outbreaks of

---

[21]Hesse M, The East Fields of Cambridge, *Proceedings of the Cambridge Antiquarian Society*, XCVI, 2007

[22]Commoners were defined as persons residing, owning or occupying land within the boundaries of the town.

plague in 1665 and 1666, temporary pest houses were built on Coldham's Common in order to isolate the victims.[23]

The figure below shows an Ordnance Survey map of Cambridge from the mid-nineteenth century. At the time, Coldham's Common was beyond the outskirts of the town, in the parish of Barnwell. The railway arrived in 1845, as shown, with Coldham's Common just to the east of the line. In 1851, a branch line was opened from Cambridge to Newmarket just north of Cambridge station, cutting through fields to the south of Coldham's Common, an area which in due course would become Romsey Town.[24] This was a significant decision, the repercussions of which will become apparent in due course.

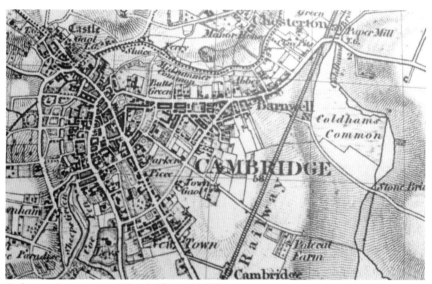

Ordnance Survey map of Cambridge, mid-1800s.

An unexpected industry developed in the vicinity of Cambridge in the 1850s – that of coprolite mining. The coprolite nodules, thought at the time to be fossilised dinosaur or animal dung, were discovered to have a high phosphate content and when treated and ground down, could be used as an agricultural fertiliser. One of the first recorded discoveries of a coprolite bed was on Coldham's Common in 1858, in the area where pits were being dug for brick-making. On the Common today, hollows and channels are still visible in various places, the remnants of coprolite digging from over 150 year ago.

[23]When the need passed these were removed in 1703.
[24]This line was subsequently extended east to Bury St Edmunds and beyond.

In 1871, the Cambridge commons' committee recommended that a lease should be granted to the Cambridgeshire Volunteers of a portion of Coldham's Common as a rifle range. For this they paid an annual rent of 5 shillings. The Ordnance Survey map of Coldham's Common from 1886 shows the rifle range extending down the length of the common, including the marked-off distances from 800 yards to 100 yards with the targets on the rifle butts sensibly at the end away from the town. Apparently, the rifle range was fenced off with iron railings.

This was the scene that Linskill would have gazed upon for the first time in early 1876. Coldham's Common was 100 acres of flat, treeless, marshy land. A drain defined the western boundary of the common, beyond which resided brickworks, some vegetable plots and the main railway line. At the very north end, there was a paper mill. Otherwise, the common was surrounded by open fields. It was bounded to the north and the west by a drain and a stream, Coldham's Brook, and on the southern boundary by a road, Coldham's Lane. Depending upon the time of year, he might have seen some cattle grazing and, perhaps, some hare coursing by local residents from nearby Barnwell. And, if the time of day was right, he might even have heard the sporadic sound of gunfire on the rifle range.

It may not have been obvious good golfing ground, except perhaps in the fertile imagination of Mr William T Linskill.

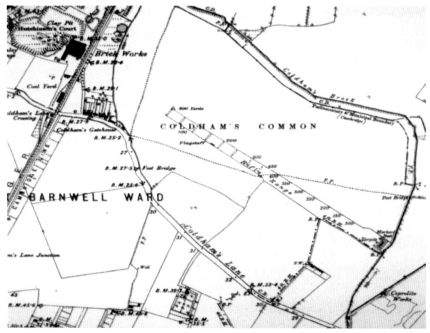

Ordnance Survey map of Coldham's Common, 1886.

Coldham Common
– the formative years

From 1876 to 1886-87

1876

Linskill's article in *The Field* on 19 February 1876 reported on the results of some of the early matches at Coldham Common. The dropping of the apostrophe and 's' is an interesting curiosity. Prior to this, Linskill had referred to Coldham's Common, which was then, and still is, the name employed for the Common. However, in all subsequent articles he refers to Coldham Common. Why drop the 's' when referring to the golf course? One possibility is that the other well-known 'inland links' courses played on common land at that time were Wimbledon, Crookham and Clapham, none of which ended with the apostrophe and 's'. Perhaps Linskill wanted Coldham to have a similar cachet? Whatever the reason, thereafter in all external and internal documentation related to the golf course, it is Coldham Common rather than Coldham's Common.

Eight golfers are mentioned by name in the 19 February article: W T Linskill, Rev Mr Wright, Rev G Pirie, Mr A J Tillyard, Mr A H Evans, Mr Waraker, Mr Matthews and Mr A H Doleman. On 11 March, *The Field* contains a further report of matches 'over the Links at Coldham during the last fortnight'. One more named player appears, Mr A W Powell. And, on 18 March a further report appears with two more players getting involved in matches, Mr C Butler and Mr H Blackburn, bringing the total to eleven.

A further interesting snippet appears in the 18 March publication. Under 'Fixtures' we read:

March 22 – Cambridge Golf Club Prize Meeting

And in the article itself, it says:

A handicap for a medal and other prizes will be held, weather permitting, on 22nd March at 2 o'clock. At present about six couples have entered.

So from this we can deduce that the Cambridge Golf Club was formed and named as such at around that time. No independently verifiable sources have been uncovered to suggest that the club existed any earlier than this. So, we must now assume that the Linskill-inspired golf club was formed in March 1876, a year after the formation of the Oxford University Golf Club which was founded in February 1875. Once again Cambridge arrives at the party a little late!

A substantial article (half a column in length) written by Linskill then appears in *The Field* on 1 April describing this momentous first meeting of the Cambridge Golf Club on Wednesday 22 March 1876. We are initially told that it was a:

> *handicap competition… for the Terminal[25] Challenge Medal, kindly presented to the Club by the Rev G Pirie (captain) together with prizes of clubs and balls.*

Thus we discover that the first captain of the new club was Reverend G Pirie and the Challenge Medal in subsequent reports would be referred to as the Pirie Medal. Reverend George Pirie came from Aberdeen, which is presumably where he had learned to play golf. He had graduated in mathematics (5th Wrangler) at Queens' in 1866. He then became a Fellow at Queens' (1866-88) and was ordained at Ely in 1869. In 1876, at the age of 32, he was also a Tutor at the college. He left Cambridge a couple of years later to return to Aberdeen where he became the Professor of Mathematics until his death in 1904.

We then learn that:

> *Owing to the indefatigable exertions of a few of the leading members, this club may now be said to be fairly set a-going, and the success of the turnout on Wednesday augurs well for its future prosperity. Although the green cannot be termed first-rate, still the club must consider itself very fortunate in securing such a suitable place for play in the neighbourhood of Cambridge.*

There is little doubt that the vast majority of the 'initial exertions' were those of the twenty-year-old Linskill. In a letter to Charles B MacDonald, Linskill wrote:

> *I had an awful job as a golf missionary there. They laughed at the idea. I taught a few chaps on Coe Fen and Sheep's Green, and then I discovered Coldham's Common. There was a rifle range there and they did coursing and*

---

[25]Terminal in this context means 'within a term'. Subsequently the competition for the Pirie Medal and other trophies was played for three times per year in the Michaelmas, Lent and Easter (or May) terms. The summer months are known as the Long Vac (vacation).

pigeon shooting – all dead against me, and an unknown and idiotic Scotch game. I had to fight the commoners and explain the game to the unsympathetic town council. They all looked on it as mad fad. At last I got it started with a few chaps, I cut the holes myself and the greens, marked the tees, mended the clubs, and made balls in an outhouse.[26]

In separate correspondence, Linskill mentioned that, in his dealings with the town corporation, they had obtained permission to play golf on Coldham Common on 2 March 1876 and that it was rent-free. However, the arrangement only allowed golf to be played between 1 October and 15 May each year. For the summer months, the course would be closed to allow cattle to graze and hay be cut. The commons' committee minute book for the period states that permission was granted on 22 February 1876 but that Mr Alexander Doleman, not Linskill, had made the written request for permission.[27]

Alexander Doleman was a more substantial golfing figure than Linskill and he was also a good bit older. He was from a golfing family from Musselburgh. He tied for ninth place in the 1870 Open Championship held at Prestwick, the year in which Young Tom Morris won by a margin of 12 shots for his third successive championship and outright possession of the Challenge Belt. Doleman had come to Cambridge in 1872 as an undergraduate aged about 36. Prior to this he had founded his own school in Blackpool. By 1877, he was again back up north as a master at Sedbergh School in Cumbria where he introduced golf to the boys. He subsequently moved back to the Blackpool area and was involved in the establishment of golf at Lytham and St Annes in the 1880s.

Returning to the first handicap meeting of the club, it was reported that:

The day was bitterly cold, and frequent showers fell; but the green being in tolerably fair condition, the play was, on the whole, good, if we consider that several of the competitors had not played golf for more than four or five weeks… When two rounds had been completed (sixteen holes) the winner turned up in A H Doleman, who completed the two rounds in 87 strokes…. Mr Doleman was in grand form, and his score is the lowest in which the rounds have yet been completed.

[26]Cameron D, *Social Links*, pp166-167, 2010
[27]The minute books are held at the Cambridgeshire Archives, Shire Hall, Cambridge.

The report said that six couples had started but that one man had failed to show up, leaving eleven competitors, all of whom had been mentioned in the earlier accounts of golf at Coldham. Their net scores were recorded as follows:

A H Doleman BA	87	(scratch)
A W Powell (Clare)	88	(29 odds)
Rev G Pirie (Queens')	93	(12 odds)
A J Tillyard (St John's)	96	(10 odds)
P Matthew (Christ's)	108	(17 odds)
C Butler	109	(14 odds)
W T Linskill	113	(scratch)
A H Evans (Clare)	114	(29 odds)
R Waraker	No score recorded	
H Blackburn (Trinity)	No score recorded	
Rev A Wright (Queens')	Retired (40 odds)	

It was noted by Linskill that his relatively poor score (for a scratch player) was accounted for by 'a run of unfortunate luck with bad-lying balls'. He also reported an amusing incident:

> *Mr R Waraker, in striking off from the first hole, missed his tee shot seven times; or, to use golfing phraseology, missed the globe seven times in succession.*

Whether Mr Waraker found this amusing is not recorded. Three more reports from Linskill appeared in *The Field* during the Easter term of 1876. A few more matches were played amongst the members but he reported that due to:

> *…the numerous exams and May festivities … golfing on Coldham Common has been rather slack.*

Perhaps his most interesting comment (15 April 1876) was:

> *In all probability, several members of the CGC will take advantage of the kind offer of the Royal North Devon Club… and make their appearance on the famous links of Westward Ho! in August next, to measure their strength with the golfers of the sister University.*

It is doubtful that this fixture took place. No report of it appeared in *The Field* and no subsequent references to such a match have been uncovered. If it had happened it would have been rather interesting if Linskill had run into George Gosset or any of his relatives while playing there. That aside, the seed of the idea of an inter-university golf match had been sown.

Towards the end of the academic year, it was reported (17 June 1876) that a contest for the championship took place between Rev Pirie, A J Tillyard and W T Linskill. After two keenly contested rounds, Linskill was the victor in the 'championship of the green'. During the summer months, Linskill was reported to be back on the links at St Andrews which would be the pattern of his life for the next twenty years.

1876-77

Michaelmas term 1876 got underway with a meeting in Reverend Pirie's rooms at Queens' on 17 October. An article in *The Field* on 4 November was important in two respects. First, the heading inferred that the club should now be known as the 'Cambridge University Golf Club' (CUGC) rather than 'Cambridge Golf Club' (CGC). And second, Linskill was elected as captain for the first time (but not the last) and it was now indicated that he had been admitted to Jesus College, although, according to the University records, he did not matriculate until Lent term 1877. The records also show that he never obtained a degree, although this was not that uncommon in those days.

The Autumn Meeting was held on 22 November with fourteen named members, although only twelve actually took part in the competition. Of the eleven who played in the first handicap competition of the club on 22 March, six were still in attendance and eight were new men. Interestingly of the new men, four were complete beginners with handicaps in the range 50-60 and the other four were off scratch, Mr Frean (Trinity), Mr Spence (Trinity), Mr Don (Trinity) and Dr Creighton (Anatomical Museum). First prize went to a Mr Dawbarn (Queens') who shot 151 for 18 holes less a handicap of 60 for a net 91. The Pirie Silver Medal was won by Reverend Pirie himself for the best scratch score of 105 (whereas it had gone to the best handicap score at the first meeting).

One further interesting comment from the Autumn Meeting was that:

> Mr Frean distanced all competitors, his drives on several occasions being very long, viz., 143, 156, 163, 164, 153, 114, 120 yards.

This gives us a sense today of how far a good golfer hit a gutta percha ball with his driver in the 1870s, and maybe also that the length of the grass and muddiness of Coldham Common did not encourage the running shot in the winter months.

At the terminal meeting of the Lent term on Wednesday 14 March 1877, fourteen players participated. A new trophy made an appearance, the Linskill Challenge Cup, kindly donated by Linskill's father, Captain Linskill. This was won by C H Spence with the best scratch score of 104. W T Linskill and P R Don tied for the handicap prize, the Pirie Medal, with a playoff to be arranged. At a meeting held that same evening, G H Frean was elected captain for the May term. It would seem at that time that the captain was appointed on a term-by-term basis. Although no longer captain, Linskill remained on the committee.

On 28 April 1877, it was reported in *The Field* that 'the club now numbers about thirty members, and that a greatly increasing interest is being shown in the game'. It was also noted that 'the grass between some of the holes is rather long, but the putting greens are in capital order'. It was decided to purchase a lawn mower and roller. On 26 May, the terminal competition of the Easter term was held. C H Spence won the Linskill Cup again with the best scratch score (108) and W T Linskill won the Pirie Handicap Medal (111). Since both players were off scratch, it suggests that the club rules at that time did not allow one player to win both trophies.

1877-78

With the new academic year commencing in October 1877 and Coldham Common open for golf again after the summer recess, the competition for the Linskill Challenge Cup and the Pirie Handicap Medal was held on 3 November. It was noted that:

Although the course usually consists of ten holes, it was resolved to only have a nine-hole course on the medal day, as the cup and medal have always been competed for over a nine-hole course.

This was not quite accurate. At the first meeting of the club on 22 March 1876, the medal was played for over an eight-hole course. Putting that to one side, Mr C H Spence won the Linskill Challenge Cup for the third time in succession, with a score of 95.

Probably the most important development was the announcement in *The Field* on 8 December 1877 that:

An Inter-University Golf Match is talked of, and Wimbledon will most probably be the green selected.

The first report of the proposed university golf match appeared in *The Field* on 2 March 1878, presumably sent in by Linskill the prime mover in setting it up:

> *There is to be an inter-University Golf Match against Oxford on Wednesday, March 6, over Wimbledon Links. Each University is to be represented by four players and no doubt the contest will be witnessed by many lovers of the noble game.*

On 9 March, a report of the match appeared in *The Field*:

> *The game consisted of four single matches, the largest aggregate of holes won to decide the match. The result was to be determined by one round of eighteen holes. Oxford was represented by Messrs. H G Hutchinson, C C C, A Stuart, W S Wilson, Exeter; C K Mackenzie, Univ. Cambridge by Messrs. W G Adams, Caius; C H Spence, Trinity; W T Linskill, Jesus; P R Don, Trinity.*

It would have been clear to the golfing readership of *The Field* that Oxford would be heavy favourites to win. Horace Hutchinson was a very fine golfer from Westward Ho! He had come up to Oxford in October 1877. Although still only 18 at the time, he had already won a number of major golfing competitions and would go on to reach the final of the first Amateur Championship in 1885 and then win the next two in 1886 and 1887. In 1908 he would become the first Englishman to be elected Captain of the R&A. He wrote extensively on golf and in particular on the technique required to play the game. It would not overstate matters to say that Horace, as he was simply known, would become one of the foremost golfing figures of that era. Alexander (Andy) Stuart was a very highly regarded scratch golfer from St Andrews and was amongst the next best in the same era as Horace Hutchinson.

The match report continued:

> *It was plain from the first that the Oxford men had the match in their own hands, as at the first hole they had scored four holes to the good. The weather was very unfavourable for golf, as a high wind was blowing all day. This told especially in the holes which are approached by narrow courses beset by threatening whins, and more than one player found plenty of work for his iron. At the turn Hutchinson (Oxford) was five up, Stuart (Oxford) five up, Wilson (Oxford) nine up, and Mackenzie (Oxford) one up. At the finish, Oxford stood twenty-four holes to the good.*

In the end Oxford won all four matches: Hutchinson won 3 up against Adams; Stuart won 5 up against Spence; Wilson won 12 up against Linskill; and Mackenzie won 4 up against Don, making the total of 24 holes up. Linskill, who had been 9 down after the first 9 holes, finished off the report with:

> For Oxford, Mr Wilson was playing in his very best form, and would have been more than a match for any of the opposite side.

A week later, Linskill wrote to *The Field* under the pseudonym 'QED' a somewhat more reflective piece:

> Sir, – Many of your readers, like myself, are delighted to see this golf match established. Year by year it will become more interesting. Though in the first year it has proved a hollow victory for Oxford, the match was highly creditable to Cambridge. Those versed in the mysteries of golf could see it was a foregone conclusion for Oxford; for that University has two "scratch players", one of them second to none in the United Kingdom, and three certainly, if not four, reared, so to speak, in the vicinity of our best golf links; while the Cambridge men are, to a certain extent, accidental golfers, who have not enjoyed the same advantages.

The general thrust of his argument in the remainder of the letter was that Oxford was 'unusually strong' and that Cambridge would get better over time as more experienced players were attracted to the University in due course.

1878-79

At a meeting held at Trinity College at the beginning of Michaelmas term 1878, Linskill was re-elected captain (for the term) and it was resolved that 'for the future, red coats should be worn as the club uniform'.

On 16 November, the Linskill Cup and Pirie Medal were played for. It was noted that a new and very hard course was laid out by the green committee (i.e. Linskill) and that the quantity of water on the links only increased its difficulty. To boot, the putting greens were very rough and heavy. Despite all of this, the number of golfers was growing, with twenty-three entrants in the competition.

On Wednesday evening, 4 December, the first dinner of CUGC took place at Trinity College. It was reported that:

> The wall over the sideboard was tastefully decorated with clubs and balls, and the members of the club all appeared in their red coats. A most pleasant evening was spent.

On 22 February 1879, there were two noteworthy items in *The Field*. It was reported that a 'resident professional was expected at the links in a few days' and that 'an iron pavilion is to be erected shortly'.

The first professional of the club was John Smith who hailed from Hoylake, the Royal Liverpool Golf Club, which had been formed in 1869. According to census records,[28] when he lived with his parents, age thirteen, in Hoylake in 1871, another occupant of the house was John Morris who was then the professional at Royal Liverpool.[29] John, or Jack Morris as he was more commonly known, was the nephew of Old Tom Morris. John Smith must have become an apprentice to Jack Morris and would have been twenty-one when he arrived at Coldham Common in 1879. Within a few weeks of his arrival, Linskill was reporting a rapid improvement in the greens and that Smith was also available to teach beginners.

The iron pavilion consisted of a club room and a workshop (for the professional) and was fitted with boxes for the members to store their equipment. It was located on the edge of Coldham Common near the railway bridge on Coldham's Lane. The fact that a club consisting of such small numbers could afford both a professional and build a club house gives some indication of the privileged background of the undergraduates in those days.

The second inter-university match took place on 20 March 1879, again at Wimbledon, but this time 6-aside. On this occasion, Cambridge exacted revenge, winning four of the six singles and the overall match by 12 holes to 2. Most surprisingly, the great Horace lost to F G H Pattison (Pembroke) 5 down. Linskill lost to Andy Stuart, but only by 1 hole. In fact, Hutchinson was drawn to comment on this many years later in his book, 'Fifty Years of Golf', published in 1919:

Then as to Andy Stuart: he had to play Linskill, and I suppose that at St Andrews, where both were practically at home, Andy would have given him a half – certainly a third would not have brought them together – for though Linskill was just about the best putter I ever saw, the rest of his game was not very formidable. They arrived at the last hole just before the Iron Hut – I can see the scene now in my mind – all even, and Linskill had the better of the hole. He was dead and Andy had quite a doubtful putt to halve the match, and I can remember a doubt arising in my own mind as to whether I wished him to hole it or not. Of course I did not want to see another match lost to Oxford, as well as my own; but still, if the news should have to go to St. Andrews that

---

[28]Cameron D, *Social Links*, p167, 2010
[29]He would remain the professional at Hoylake for 60 years.

Andy had been beaten by Linskill, level, it would be such a fine joke that it was almost worth the lost match. However he holed that putt with the courage of a lion – he was always a good putter at the last putt of a match – and so the match was halved.

Hutchinson's recall was not quite accurate. The putt holed by Stuart won him the match. However, he was inferring that Linskill was closer to a 9 handicapper in comparison with a scratch player of Stuart's standing.

On 10 May 1879, it was reported that CUGC would play its first club match at Coldham Common the following Saturday. This was to be a 6-aside match against the Wimbledon-based London Scottish club. Unfortunately, no report of the match appeared in *The Field* so we cannot be certain that it proceeded.

1879-80

The undergraduate golfers of the late 1870s were hardy types. When the terminal competition for the Linskill Cup and Pirie Handicap Medal were played for on Saturday 22 November 1879, Linskill reported in *The Field* that:

The whole affair was, if any such thing can be imagined, a very excellent specimen of what golf would be if played in the region of the North Pole. Snow lay thick all over the course, and the cold was intense, the snow freezing on the balls and on the faces of the clubs; and in some places the teeing grounds were so slippery, that standing was by no means easy.

Amazingly, there were twenty-three entrants that day and it was reported that 'Mr W Welsh had carried off the Linskill Cup with a magnificent score of 98; Mr Pattison being second in 100, won the Pirie Medal.'

William Welsh was born in Edinburgh in 1859. At the age of fifteen, he entered the university there and made his mark in mathematics, classics and other branches of study. In 1879, he was admitted to Jesus College at Cambridge and won the chief scholarship 'with almost phenomenal marks'. In 1882, he obtained a BA in mathematics as the Senior Wrangler and in the following year won the Smith Prize, the top award in mathematics. In 1884 he became a fellow of Jesus. The Master of the college at the time said that Welsh could have gone to the top of any profession that he could have chosen to adopt. Instead, he remained at Jesus as a fellow and tutor for the rest of his life. Outside of teaching, golf was his passion playing at Brancaster and Royston. Although he had the ability to play in major competitions, he never did, preferring a quieter life. He became President of CUGC in 1896 and remained in that position for twenty-nine years. Upon his death, while playing golf at Brancaster in 1925, a subscription was raised, largely amongst past members, to fund a trophy which was presented to the club in his memory. The Welsh Cup remains in the possession of the club to this day.

In March 1880, Welsh, playing off scratch, repeated his success in winning the Linskill Cup, this time in better conditions with a score of 95. Welsh also won the top match in the Varsity match (once again held on Wimbledon Common) against A R Paterson. However, his was the only success and the overall result was 9 holes to 1 in favour of Oxford. Linskill, still the Cambridge captain, did not play on this occasion 'having met with an accident'. The report (presumably by Linskill) noted rather presumptuously that:

> *The match was very close, and had this gentleman played it is highly probable it would have been even closer.*

Back at Coldham Common, while the winter weather created its challenges for the golfers, new ones arose as summer approached. On 1 May 1880 it was reported that while the grass was short, 'the daisies render it rather difficult to find the balls'. It did not seem to be a problem for William Welsh who won the Linskill Cup to complete a clean sweep in the academic year, this time with an astonishing score of 84, 10 shots better than the next man.

1880-81

An early report in November 1880 noted that, 'The club is rapidly increasing in numbers and popularity'. There were twenty-two participants for the Cup and Medal in the Michaelmas term played in heavy rain, which resulted in the greens being 'fairly flooded'. Probably to no-one's great surprise, William Welsh won for a fourth time in succession with a score of 90 for the eighteen holes.

The heavy conditions on Coldham Common were challenging enough for the golfers. However, additional difficulties arose as local youths realised that there were financial rewards to be made from what became known as 'mudding'. The boys would hang around waiting for a ball to be hit in their general direction then, on seeing it land, press it into the mud. They would then seek payment to help find it, or sell it on to another golfer coming through later. This was becoming commonplace as a case before the Cambridge Borough Police Court demonstrated. It was reported in *The Cambridge Independent Press* that John Stearn, age 17, was charged with stealing a golf ball of value 3d from H J H Fenton, MA on Coldham Common. The report contained the following exchanges:

> *The Magistrates' Clerk: I presume, Mr Fenton, that pressing the ball into the mud is not part of the game of golf?*

Witness: Certainly not.

This boy, he said, was certainly no worse than many others, but he saw dozens of them every time he played. He took up the matter wholly on public grounds, to try to stop this nuisance, which is a disgrace to society.

Stearn, who was unemployed, was found guilty and fined 2/6d, to be paid by his father.

It must have been a very trying winter as no further reports of matches appeared until 19 March 1881 when, more importantly, it was announced that:

In consequence of the wet weather, and the teams being unable to practice, the Oxford and Cambridge match is put off.

Apart from the war years of 1915-19 and 1940-45, this is the only other occasion in which the Varsity match has been cancelled since it commenced.

On 28 May 1881, it was reported that W Welsh had maintained his form, winning the Linskill Cup for the sixth time in succession (which implies that, although not reported on, he had also won it in the Lent term).

1881-82

At the beginning of the new academic year in October 1881, an upbeat report appeared in *The Field*:

This club is progressing favourably. John Smith, the professional, has greatly extended the round this term, and improved the putting greens.

The most significant news to report in the Michaelmas term was that William Welsh failed to win the Linskill Cup, having won it on all previous occasions he had entered. He fell one shot shy, scoring 102 to R C Faithfull's 101 on a newly lengthened nine-hole course. A seemingly insignificant footnote appeared in reports of matches during the winter months – a Major Gardner was mentioned to have participated.

A few days ahead of the Varsity match in March 1882, the club's members competed for the Linskill Cup and Pirie Medal. William Welsh was back to winning ways, taking the Linskill Cup with a score of 96 in strong winds.

The Varsity match in 1882 was the tightest yet, with Cambridge winning by 8 holes to 7. In the top match Horace Hutchinson beat William Welsh by 3 holes. Interestingly, of the six matches played two were won by each side and two were halved. Perhaps somewhat controversially, the aforementioned Major Gardner played in the bottom match. In the reports of the match in *The Field*, where normally a player's college would be denoted, Major C H Gardner's name is followed in parenthesis by '12th Regiment'.[30] It is noted in *Fifty Years of Sport at Oxford, Cambridge and the Great Public Schools*, arranged by Lord Desborough and published in 1913:

> But next year [1882] evidence was afforded that sophistication was far from complete. Linskill, still Captain of the CUGC, being disappointed by one of his chosen side, filled his place by roping in Major Gardner, who was acting with great acceptance as adjutant of the Cambridge Volunteers. The substitute did great work by holing a nice putt on the last green to halve his match, his team being at that time one hole to the good.

If any further confirmation of Major Gardner's status (or non-status) was required, it appeared in the article below the Varsity match report in *The Field* on 11 March 1882 where it was noted that 'Major Gardner (Non Coll)' had been elected onto the CUGC committee. In the *Alumni Cantabrigienses*, Charles Henry Gardner is reported to have matriculated in Michaelmas term 1881. His status is given as 'Non-College'. No other information is supplied.

A sense of *déjà vu* was experienced in the Easter term – the grass was too long for good play, the common was a mass of buttercups and William Welsh secured the Linskill Cup for an eighth time.

1882-83

As the new term started the most important news was that John Smith, the professional, had been replaced by J O F Morris. James Ogilvy Fairley Morris was the son of Old Tom Morris and the younger brother of Young Tom Morris (who had died tragically in 1875 at the age of 24). JOF, as he was known, had also become a golf professional but was never as successful as his father or brother. His best result in the Open Championship was a creditable third place five years earlier in 1878 at Prestwick. Although he was obviously still a very good golfer, club-making was his speciality. Early reports from Coldham Common said that 'there is enough work for six men mending clubs'.

If not quite six men, three were reported to be *in situ* in November 1882 – Morris, Bob Martin and S Youngman. Nothing is known of S Youngman but Bob Martin of St Andrews won the Open Championship in 1876 (and would go on to do so again in 1885). Subsequently, in December, it was reported that Bob Martin had been appointed clubmaker and professional in place of JOF who had returned to St Andrews to work as the foreman in his father's workshop.

---

[30]The 12th Regiment of Foot was originally the Suffolk Regiment. Cambridgeshire was incorporated into the regiment in 1873. The headquarters of the regiment were in Bury St Edmunds.

The Michaelmas terminal competition of 1882 had the largest entry yet at 28 participants. Once again William Welsh returned the lowest gross score of 89. However, the report says that Mr Welsh had decided not to enter the Linskill Cup so it was awarded to the next best, Mr J L Casson (Trinity), who 'was playing a capital game' and shot 92. Perhaps Welsh felt that winning the Linskill Cup eight times was quite enough!

In advance of the Lent term, it was reported that:

> *A new and extended course has been laid out, and the greens are levelled and rolled by Bob Martin, professional. The actual distance of the two rounds, or eighteen holes, is about four miles.*[31]

It was also reported that, 'in spite of the wind and weather, there is a large muster of red coats every afternoon'.

When the Linskill Cup and the Pirie Handicap Medal were played for on 21 February 1883, there was no William Welsh in the field and the Linskill Cup was won by none other than W T Linskill himself with a score of 95.

The 1883 Varsity match proved to be a close run thing again, with Oxford winning by 15 holes up to 13 up in the first 8-aside match. It is interesting to note that Cambridge actually won four of the matches to Oxford's three (the top match between Linskill and Sir Ludovic Grant was halved). J A Dun's victory over W P Frean by 9 holes materially turned the result in Oxford's favour.

After the match, and after luncheon at the Royal Wimbledon golf club, the Cambridge team made their way back to King's Cross in a 'four-in-hand'.[32] Linskill reported that this caused an unusual stir at King's Cross and they also received unexpected ovations from the public along the way. He subsequently realised that they had been mistaken for Cambridge's rowing representatives. As he put it:

> *They were eight in number, an eight-oared boat came up by the same train, they wore knickerbockers, they drove in a four-in-hand over Putney Bridge only a few hours before the crew were expected; these facts, added to the presence of a correspondent of one of the leading journals on the return journey, all seemed to aid in favour of this delusion.*

The 1883 Boat Race, in fact, took place two weeks after the Varsity golf match. Oxford won that one too.

---

[31]The four miles must have referred to the total distance walked rather than the measured length of the holes – see the final section of this chapter on the nine-hole course. Alternatively, Linskill simply over-estimated.

[32]A four-in-hand is a carriage drawn by a team of four horses having the reins rigged in such a way that it can be driven by a single driver.

1883-84

When the links re-opened in October 1883, Bob Martin was still 'the resident clubmaker and professional'. It was also noted that, 'In addition to the pavilion, a new club room will be opened shortly'. On 1 November, at a General Meeting, the officers were elected for the term. It was reported that:

> *A unanimous vote of thanks was accorded to Mr W T Linskill on his retirement from the post of captain, for the very energetic spirit he had always shown in the affairs of the club, and for the way in which he had performed his arduous duties.*

Linskill, the leading light at Cambridge, had been captain for seven years, every term since Michaelmas 1876, with the exception of the May term in 1877 when G M Frean was captain. He never completed his degree and perhaps this signalled that he never would. Mr E F Chance (Gonville and Caius) was unanimously elected to be the new captain for the Lent term of 1884.

The Linskill Cup was played for in fine weather in November 1883 and 'the putting greens were considered better than at any previous time in the existence of the links'. However, membership numbers seemed to be down somewhat – only 18 took part and none were off scratch.

Although it had been announced that a match was arranged against London Scottish, to take place on 17 May 1879, a report of that match never appeared in *The Field*. However, in November 1883, CUGC played two matches, one against Felixstowe (formed in 1880) away and the other against Great Yarmouth (formed in 1882) at home. This latter match was therefore the first documented fixture to be held at Coldham Common. While membership numbers at the club might have been down, it did not stop CUGC winning comprehensively – 24 holes up against Felixstowe and 48 holes up against Great Yarmouth. Home and away matches with these two clubs became regular fixtures in subsequent years.

When the return match against Felixstowe was played at Coldham Common on 8 March 1884, a match was arranged between the clubs' two professionals – and what a star billing it was! Bob Martin, the CUGC professional, and winner of the Open Championship in 1876 played against the Felixstowe professional, Willie Fernie, 'the present holder of the champion cup'. In front of a large turnout of spectators, the two pros (both from St Andrews) put on a superlative exhibition of golf with Martin winning by two holes, shooting 78 versus Fernie's 81. Such low scoring had not been seen before at Coldham Common for the round of 18 holes.

By way of comparison, J C Wilson (scratch) had won the Linskill Cup two weeks prior with a score of 89. Linskill's match report, which appeared in *The Field* on 15 March 1884, is shown below.

The University match at Wimbledon Common was yet again a close affair with Oxford winning by 18 holes to 16.

PROFESSIONAL MATCH.—After lunch the chief interest centred in a professional match between Bob Martin, ex-champion and C.U.G.C. professional, and W. Fernie, present holder of the champion cup, and Felixstowe professional, both St. Andrews men. Fernie took the honour, and led off with a long straight drive; Martin was not quite so far, and failed to be up with his iron, while Fernie pitched over the green into rough grass, the hole eventually being halved in 5 strokes. The second hole fell to Martin in 4 against Fernie's 5. The next hole Fernie holed in 3, while Martin missed his put, and took a 4. The next hole both men holed in 5. At the next hole both drives lay close to the green, and Fernie laid his iron shot dead, holing in 3 to Martin's 4. At the sixth hole, Martin played a beautiful niblick shot, laying his ball dead, and holed in 3 to Fernie's 5. The long hole was halved in 6, and the next one halved in 5. The ninth hole was well played and halved in 4, each player holing a long put. Thus, at the end of the first round, the match stood all square. The first hole of the second round was halved in 4, while at the next hole Fernie failed to be up with his iron, and Martin won the hole in 4 to Fernie's 5. At the third hole both men drove good shots, but Fernie, laying his iron shot dead, holed out in 3 to Martin's 4. The fourth hole was halved in 5, while at the next, Fernie failed to hole a short put, only holing in 5 to Martin's 4. At the sixth hole, Fernie drove over the green, and Martin far to the right; however, Bob, by one of his niblick pitches, lay dead, and holed in 3 to Fernie's 4. At the seventh hole, Martin had to play two more on the green, but holing a long put, stole a half in 5, thus making him dormy. At the eighth hole, Fernie lay dead in 3, but Martin, putting down another long put, halved the hole. The next hole was halved in 5. Martin thus won a keenly contested match by two holes. Fernie's long straight driving, and Martin's extraordinary skill with his iron niblick. were greatly admired. W. T. Linskill acted as umpire. The following is the detailed score :

First round	{ Martin—5	4	4	5	4	3	6	5	4	—	40
	{ Fernie—5	5	3	5	3	5	6	5	4	—	41
Second round	{ Martin—4	4	4	5	4	3	5	4	5	—	38
	{ Fernie—4	5	3	5	5	4	5	4	5	—	40

Total—Martin, 78; Fernie, 81.

Match report in *The Field*, Bob Martin versus Willie Fernie, past and present Open Champions, at Coldham Common on 8 March 1884.

1884-85

When the links re-opened again in October 1884, Bob Martin had departed and Frank Park from Musselburgh was now reported to be the resident professional and clubmaker. Frank Park was one of the sons of Willie Park Senior, who won the first Open Championship in 1860 as well as on three other occasions. Frank was also the brother of Willie Park Jr, who would win the Open twice, in 1887 and 1889 and go on to be a prestigious golf course designer in the UK and in America. In November, it was reported that Park, 'by daily rolling the putting greens, has got them into better condition than has been known since the club was established'.

The stand-out player in this period was J C Wilson (Jesus). On 24 February 1885, he won the Linskill Cup for the fifth time in succession with a gross 98. Wilson's net 98 (since he was playing off scratch) was also good enough for him to tie for third place in the Pirie Handicap Medal with a Colonel Hough (Trinity), who shot 163 off a handicap of 65!

On 6 February 1885, it was noted in the House of Commons' Committee minute book that:

> *..the Sub-committee be requested to meet the Parliamentary Committee on Friday next as to the Ipswich, Felixstowe and Midlands Railway requiring a piece of Coldham's Common.*

A Bill was drafted and debated in the House of Commons in May 1886, but it did not proceed. However, this was a portent of things to come regarding the railways and Coldham Common.

No report of the 1885 University match appeared in *The Field*. It had been played on 12 March with Oxford winning resoundingly by 39 holes to 1. Perhaps Linskill felt that there was nothing more to add?

1885-86

In October 1885, it was noted that 'some of the members of the CUGC are trying to lay out a links at Therfield Heath, near Royston, on the GNR, where an excellent round might be obtained'. Whether Linskill knew that Andrew Graham Murray and George Gosset *et al* had done the very same thing in 1869 is not known. In any case, it came to nothing. In February 1886 it was noted that although a fine long round of eighteen holes could be played, permission to do so had not been granted.

On 17 February 1886, seventeen members took part in the Linskill Cup at Coldham Common. The club captain, Herbert B Boyd won with a score of 86. Further down the field, F Darwin shot 114 (less 14, net 100). This was Francis Darwin, son of Charles and father of Bernard. Frank Darwin, as he was more commonly known, had gone to Trinity and graduated in natural sciences in 1870. After studying medicine in London he returned to Down House in Kent, where he had been born, to work with his father in the field of botany. After Charles Darwin died in 1882, Frank returned to Cambridge where he became a reader in botany. In 1886 he was 38 years of age. He had learned to play golf at Aberdovey in Wales where his brother-in-law, Arthur Ruck had laid out a small course on the linksland in 1882. His son Bernard, who was born in 1876 had received his first golf club in 1884 and probably played his first golf shots at Cambridge 'on the unspeakably muddy and unsavoury course on Coldham Common.'[33]

[33]Darwin B, *The World That Fred Made*, London, 1955

The 1886 Varsity match went a similar way to 1885, Oxford winning by 37 holes. In five of the eight matches played Cambridge were only a total of 4 holes down, but unfortunately the other three matches were lost at a cost of 33 holes! On this occasion, Linskill almost certainly did write the match report in *The Field* (13 March, 1886). After the Varsity match was concluded, an informal foursome was arranged in which Linskill played. He noted at the end of the article:

> *The wants of the Light Blues were well looked after by Linskill, who was prevented from representing his 'Varsity through having taken his degree beyond the stipulated time.*

It would have been a little more accurate to say that he had not completed his degree at all.

1886-87

When the links at Coldham Common were open again in October 1886, it was reported that, 'thanks to the exertions of Frank Park, the greens are greatly enlarged and improved'. It was subsequently noted that, 'sea sand has greatly improved the putting greens'. It was also noted that 'the long course will be used this term, the two rounds or eighteen holes covering a distance of more than four miles'.

As well as Linskill and Frank Darwin, William Welsh could be found playing in a match there from time to time. Interest in golf seemed to be on the increase; it was reported that twenty-six new members had been elected during the Michaelmas term. For the Lent term, a familiar name appeared as secretary of the club, W T Linskill.

Whether he was passing through, or paying a visit, Willie Dunn 'of North Berwick' played a match at Coldham Common in November 1886 against Park and Linskill. Willie Dunn was actually born in Blackheath where his father Willie Dunn Senior, had been 'keeper of the green'. In 1886, he was the professional at Westward Ho!. He is perhaps best known for designing some of the early golf courses in America, including the extension of Shinnecock Hills from twelve to eighteen holes.

The Varsity match went ahead as usual in March at Wimbledon Common. After losing the previous four contests, Cambridge were the victors in the 1887 match, 12 holes up. However, the most significant event of the year was not the outcome of the battle against Oxford; it was the outcome of the battle against the Great Eastern Railway Company (GER). The GER proposed to alter the route of its line from Cambridge to Newmarket (and points east) so that it cut through the heart of Coldham's Common. There was opposition to this – the Commons Preservation Society, the Cambridgeshire Volunteer Rifle Corp and, needless to say, the Cambridge University Golf Club. The town corporation also seemed to be against it. Linskill wrote to the President of CUGC, Augustus Austin Leigh who at that time was the Vice Provost of King's College, to encourage him to lobby relevant MPs in the House of Commons.

The debate on an amendment to the Great Eastern Railway Bill specifically associated with Coldham's Common appears in Hansard, dated 28 April 1887.[34] Arguments for and against were put forward. One of the main arguments against the amendment was recorded as follows:

> *So far as the recreation of the people is concerned, the only persons who are really interested in this Common, in connection with playing games upon it, are some 60 members of the University, who have the use of the Common from the Corporation for nothing, and play golf upon it. They are the only persons who can possibly suffer by the severance of the Common, and surely if they want a golf ground they are able to provide one at their own expense....*
> *I deny, however, that the interests of 60 members of the University of Cambridge should interfere with a great public improvement like this.*

In the end, the amendment was approved and the golf course at Coldham Common was 'saved'. At the CUGC EGM in May 1887, a vote of thanks was recorded to various Members of Parliament for the actions they had taken in the House to prevent the proposed encroachment of the railway.

On the same day as the EGM, the Linskill Cup and Pirie Handicap medal were played in excellent conditions in which twenty members took part. After the day's golf, it was further reported that:

> *A large meeting of the club was held in the evening, and, in consequence of the great increase of the membership, it was resolved to enlarge and improve the present University Golf Pavilion before the October term.*

The 9-hole course at Coldham Common

From 1876 to 1887, Coldham Common was a 9-hole course, although strictly speaking, at the very outset when the first competition was played on 22 March 1876, it consisted of only eight holes. On 18 November 1876, a report in *The Field* noted that the Coldham Common course had been extended from eight to

[34]A general enabling bill.

nine holes with the new hole located in the vicinity of two ditches, 'and therefore requires careful manipulation'. The two ditches are likely to have been at the east end of the common where Coldham's Brook and a water-filled ditch exist (possibly created during the era of coprolite mining that once took place on the common).

From time to time the course was altered or lengthened although little detail was provided. The course (for two rounds of nine holes) varied in reports from 3 to 4 miles in length (probably including the walk between greens and tees).

In *The Field* on 1 November 1884, a brief description of the 9-hole course at that time appeared:

> *The course has.... been extended, and there are now three very long holes – namely, the third, the sixth, and the last. The first five holes have not been altered, but the old sixth is missed out; therefore, teeing off from the fifth hole, one plays to what was the seventh, and it takes three good drives and an iron shot to reach it. The next hole is on the old green, but, instead of now turning homewards, a new hole has been made over the ditch by the brickworks and just short of the mill dam – a decided improvement as it affords an excellent hazard. The ditch is re-crossed in return to the home hole, which is a very long one.*

The most insightful view we have of the 9-hole course was provided in 1887 when a map of Coldham's Common was prepared as part of the debate regarding the GER railway line cutting through the common.

The map opposite shows the common, consisting of an area of 98 acres 1 rood and 36 poles,[35] together with details of its surroundings. This includes the location of the golf pavilion in 1887 on the south-west corner near the entrance to the common. It also shows details within the common, including the rifle range, footpaths, the proposed railway line and nine red dots indicating the location of the greens for the 9-hole course.

On closer inspection of the map, it might seem surprising to see the 1st green located near the pavilion (and the 9th green somewhat distant from it). The normal scheme of things would have the finishing hole (i.e. the 9th green) closest to the clubhouse. However, in a letter written by Linskill, lobbying against the proposed GER railway line, he added a postscript which stated, 'you will notice the holes are wrongly numbered'. So, logically this would suggest that the 2nd green on the map is the 1st, the 3rd is the 2nd, etc., resulting in the home green being the 9th instead of the 1st as shown on the map.

[35] 1 rood = 1/4 acre; 1 pole = 1/40 rood.

The flow of the holes is anti-clockwise around the common. Using *Google Earth*, the holes are estimated to have had the following yardages:

1	260
2	320
3	440
4	210
5	160
6	220
7.	200
8	360
9	300
Total:	2,470

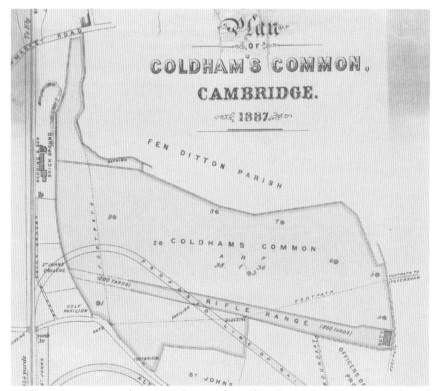

Coldham Common map from 1887 showing the golf pavilion and the nine holes indicated by red dots.

It is interesting to compare the description that appeared in *The Field* in November 1884 with the map showing the 9-hole course in 1887. In 1884, it was noted that there were now three very long holes (as a result of changes implemented), the 3rd, the 6th and the 9th. In 1887, the 3rd was 440 yards long but that the 6th and 9th were only 220 and 300 yards respectively. In 1884 the new (long) 6th was created by missing out the old 6th green and playing from the 5th green to the 7th green. If this was done, it would have create a hole of about 410 yards. The 1884 new 7th would be the same hole as designated as the 8th in 1887 (i.e. 360 yards). The two final new holes in 1884 are the 8th which would go to the north end of the common over the ditch towards the brickworks (about 240 yards), leaving a very long 9th (about 530 yards) back to the pavilion. Overall this longer course in 1884 would have measured 2,930 yards, nearly 500 yards longer than the 1887 course.

There are two possible explanations for the above. It could have been that the new extended course, as described in *The Field* in 1884, proved to be a failure and the club reverted back to the older, shorter course that is shown on the 1887 map. Perhaps the long holes were considered too tedious in the winter with poor run using the gutta percha ball. Alternatively, the layout shown on the 1887 map may actually be the course as it was prior to 1884. Whichever is the correct interpretation, the map in all likelihood shows the course as it was at a time prior to 1887, probably also before 1884, and possibly even back to when it was first laid out in the mid-1870s.

6

Coldham Common
– the halcyon days

From 1887-88 to 1895-96

1887-88

When golf re-started in the Michaelmas term of 1887, the alterations to the pavilion had been carried out and 'add considerably to the comfort of Members'. Linskill was still the secretary and Frank Park the professional, although the latter was now assisted by James Gourlay from St Andrews. Gourlay would go on to become a well-known clubmaker. In late October it was announced that:

> *This club is increasing so very rapidly in numbers and popularity, that it has become necessary to lay out an eighteen hole course (instead of the present nine hole course), of fully four and a half miles in extent.*

Four weeks later, the work had been carried out:

> *…several hazards have been added, and the new putting greens, though not yet first rate, are, thanks to the exertions of our professionals, Park and Gourlay, in very creditable order.*

For the first competition played on the new 18-hole course shortly thereafter, for the Linskill Cup and Pirie handicap medal, there were twenty-five entrants. Interestingly, twenty-two of them were from Trinity.

Owing to the influx of new members, the alterations to the pavilion the previous summer did not prove sufficient and so it had to be expanded yet again, in fact doubled in size, during the Christmas vacation.

The Lent terminal competition, held on Friday 17 February 1888 had only sixteen participants owing to the weather. Linskill reported that:

> *The day was bitterly cold, and deep snow lay in the hollows, while the frost of the previous evening had rendered the putting greens very uncertain. During play several sharp showers of hail and snow fell. There was a large muster of golfers in the pavilion, but many seemed to prefer the friendly warmth of the fire to playing in the polar weather outside.*

Always the optimist, Linskill reported in *The Cambridge Review* that 'with careful play, and the use of red balls, there was plenty of interest for the keen golfer'. Perhaps the gross winning score for the Linskill Cup of 105 by F N Fischer was not so bad under the circumstances.

The very next day, Cambridge entertained Felixstowe at the appropriately-named Coldham Common. In 'blinding snow showers and intense cold' the home team won by 27 holes up. Another match between the clubs' professionals was played. On this occasion, Jack Thomson of Felixstowe comfortably beat CUGC's Frank Park, 6 up with 4 holes to play. Linskill commented on the match:

> *Coming in, Park more or less broke down, especially in his putting, missing several easy shots. His driving was on the whole very fine, but his iron play was weak, being constantly either short or past the green. Thomson played a steady game throughout, with occasional brilliant shots, the lofting of a stimy at the fourth hole evoking much applause.*

The following Saturday, Cambridge maintained their cold-weather form, beating Oxford at Wimbledon Common, this time by 20 holes to 12. The bottom match proved to be rather crucial for Cambridge, with A R H Smith winning 9 holes up.

In March, the weather must have improved because some low scores on the 18-hole course were reported. William Welsh, on a rare outing, shot 79 which shortly thereafter was matched by Linskill himself. But both these scores were eclipsed by the professional John Lambert 'who accomplished the round in the wonderful score of 74, perfect play'.

1888-89

After four years at Coldham Common, Frank Park had departed and was replaced by John Lambert of Musselburgh with James Gourlay as his assistant. Lambert had come 12th in the 1886 Open Championship at Musselburgh.

At a meeting of the club in early October 1888, 39 new members were elected. Interestingly in the same edition of *The Field* (3 November 1888), it was reported under the headline 'Cambridge Ladies Golf Club' that:

> *A ladies' golf course has been started in the University town, and a capital nine-hole green laid out on Coldham Common to the right of the long outgoing course. Already fourteen members have joined, and its success looks most promising.*

It is doubtful that this was the case, as no further reports appeared.

Twenty-nine golfers participated in the terminal competition on 16 November 1888, one of the largest entries seen. Although he finished well down the field shooting 97 less 6 for a net 91, there was one conspicuous new member, H S Colt. He was also elected onto the committee at an extraordinary general meeting held at Linskill's home at 48 New Square, Cambridge that evening.

Harry Shapland Colt was born in Highgate, London in 1869. After schooling at Monkton Combe near Bath where he excelled at sports, he went up to Cambridge in 1887. On completing his BA in Law, he went into practice at a Hastings-based firm. During his time there, he helped to design Rye and became its honorary secretary in 1895. In 1897, he became a founder member of the R&A's Rules of Golf Committee. In 1901, he applied for the job of secretary at the newly established Sunningdale club and amongst 400 applicants, he was the successful candidate. It was from this base that he gradually developed his interest and ultimately his career as a golf course architect. Colt, together with his partners Charles Alison, John Morrison, and for a few earlier years Dr Alister MacKenzie, was involved in the design, construction, and remodelling of over 300 courses world-wide including Sunningdale New, the Eden Course at St Andrews, Royal Portrush in Ireland, and Pine Valley and Augusta in the USA. Colt himself was directly responsible for 115 of these.

As well as the matches against Felixstowe and Great Yarmouth, a first match was played on 8 December 1888 at (the already Royal) Cromer, a 9-hole course very recently opened on the north-east Norfolk coast. In thick fog, 'with balls, struck by unseen players, whizzing through the mist, while shouts of "Fore!" were heard on all sides', Cambridge won by 22 holes. In February 1889, another new fixture appeared – against the Royal Engineers Golf Club. The opposition consisted of three captains, three lieutenants, two majors and a colonel. In the top match, Captain Dumbleton beat Linskill by one hole; otherwise they lost 33 holes down. Dumbleton would be posted to Hong Kong shortly thereafter and was the architect of the first golf course there.

Oxford won the Varsity match in March 1889 at Wimbledon by 18 holes to 9. A couple of interesting, although unrelated, asides appeared in Linskill's piece in *The Field*:

> *Oxford came by train; Cambridge, as is their custom, by four horse coach from London.*

> *To prove what I said about golf becoming more popular every year, there are at the present moment over two hundred golfers at each University.*

At the terminal competition in May 1889, played in 'long, rank grass and daisies', only two players in the field broke 100 with Mr Alistair Clark (Jesus) winning the Linskill Cup with a score of 93. At the EGM held that evening at Linskill's house, Mr Clark 'kindly offered a prize of £2.10s. for each of the October and Lent terms, to go to the winner of the four best aggregate scores in the weekly handicaps'.[36]

Also at the EGM, the Reverend Augustus Austen Leigh, the provost of King's, stepped down as President of the club, with Francis Darwin (Trinity) elected in his place. H S Colt (Clare) was elected captain for the year ahead.

1889-90

'The 'Varsity links at Coldham Common' re-opened in October 1889 with Lambert and Gourlay 'hard at work on the greens'. However, this did not last long as it was reported in the CUGC minutes on 6 December that Lambert had resigned suddenly. James Gourlay made an offer to take over from the beginning of the Lent term and this was accepted by the committee. His offer included the provision of 'ready made clubs from Tom Morris of St Andrews and Peter Fernie of Wimbledon'.

It was also reported that drainage had greatly improved the 18-hole course. This transpired to be an overly rosy picture (perhaps not for the first time), as the Linskill Cup and Pirie Medal, competed for on 21 November, 'owing to the flooded state of the land' had to be played on the 9-hole course 'which is always dry'. After a play-off, H S Colt won the Linskill Cup. The Clark Prize, for the four best aggregate scores in the weekly handicap competitions in the Michaelmas term, had its first winner in C C Davie off a handicap of 11.

On 23 January 1890, *The Cambridge Review* included an editorial piece on the ongoing drainage issue at Coldham Common (presumably drafted by Linskill). The gist of it was that the 9-hole course was on relatively dry land but that the 18-hole course regularly suffered from waterlogging. Because of the influx of new members, the club needed the 18-hole course to ensure that everyone who wanted to play could. The Coldham Commoners were not interested in paying for drainage as their prime concern was for lush grassland for their cattle to enjoy in the summer months. So who would pay for it?

On 19 February 1890, the Lent term cup and medal competition took place. Colt again tied for the Linskill Cup but on this occasion there is no record of a play-off. At the 'usual' EGM that evening when the officers for the forthcoming Easter term were elected, rather surprisingly Colt stepped down as captain and Cecil A Cancellor (Trinity Hall) was elected for the forthcoming Easter term.

---

[36]This was a not inconsiderable prize, worth about £250 in today's money.

This was unusual. Since 1877-78 (with the exception of 1883-84, when Linskill, E F Chance and E Armitage were captain for one term each), although elected on a term-by-term basis, there had always been one captain per academic year. In any case, 'a hearty vote of thanks was proposed to Mr H S Colt, the retiring captain, for his energetic services during his tenure of office'.

At the EGM, it was also announced that a new 'Club Medal' would be competed for on a handicap basis on 11 March. The medal was described as:

> *Very handsome, and is made by Morris of King's Parade. On one side are the University arms and motto, and on the other St Andrew on the Cross. At the top are crossed clubs, bearing a scroll on which is inscribed 'Far and Sure'.*

The first winner was E D Chetham Strode with a score of 105-18=87. This Club Medal was subsequently renamed the St Andrews Medal in December 1890. The Varsity match at Royal Wimbledon golf club took place on 4 March. Colt played in the top match, captaining the side; Cancellor, who was due to replace him, did not participate. It was reported that:

> *The day was bitterly cold, a keen frost prevailed, and snow from one to two inches deep lay all over the course, rendering play extremely difficult and flukey. The putting greens were clear for a few feet around each hole, and approaching was certainly the most difficult part of the game, a ball pitched short sticking in the heaped snow, and a ball alighting on the swept portion racing merrily into the mound of snow beyond. Red balls and forecaddies were absolutely necessary.*

The flukiness of the conditions might have had a material effect on the result. Cambridge won by one hole; 15 up against 14 up in the eight matches played. Possibly to its chagrin, Oxford won four of the matches to Cambridge's three, with the top match halved.

Back at Coldham Common, flooding problems continued to plague the 18-hole course to the extent that permission was sought (and finally given by the Commons Committee) to install drainage. In the end, via subscription and donations from its members, CUGC raised the necessary £35 to install drains 'in every direction'. In today's money, this would amount to around £4,000 providing, once again, an indication of the affluence of the undergraduate members of the club. On 5 April 1890, it was reported that:

> *All the ground (now a perfect lake) where the first three holes, of the eighteen hole course, lie is being thoroughly and deeply drained from the rifle range railings to the road, as also the wet ground in the neighbourhood of the thirteenth, fifteenth, seventeenth and eighteenth holes.*

If that was not bad enough, it was noted in the club minutes (19 February) that:

> *It was agreed that the muddy holes at the corner of each of the Rifle Range palings be counted as Hazards, the penalty for lifting a ball being one stroke.*

In an article in *The Field* in May 1891 it was commented that 'in the future the Cambridge eighteen-hole course will be as dry as any other inland green can possibly be'. It remained to be seen if this would be the case.

1890-91

The rapid growth in numbers was not only putting a strain on the golf course. Despite several extensions the clubhouse was also becoming increasingly cramped. At the start of the new term in October 1890 it was reported that, 'Members are pouring in so very rapidly, that considerable additions are to be made to the club pavilion'. In fact at the 'usual Extraordinary General Meeting' on 31 October, in the light of the fact that 93 new members had joined that term, it was agreed to erect 'a commodious new clubhouse'.

However, there were voices of caution. One member, George Townsend-Warner (Jesus) took to the letters pages of *The Cambridge Review*:

> *Although the club has a promising future, there are practically no funds at hand. Whatever expense is incurred… will chiefly come on future members to pay off. Hence it is I think our duty to be prudent and not to buy more land than we absolutely want for a clubhouse… . But if, though heaven may avert the day, Coldham Common were no longer available; if the GER succeeded in its evil designs, or the town for some reason, withdrew its permission; then we should find that the less unnecessary we owned the better."*

There were also other problems afoot. The caddies were agitating – they wanted 'a shilling a round instead of eighteenpence'. In *The Cambridge Review* it was commented that in the olden days a demand of this nature would have been met by a refusal, in turn by a strike, and in turn by members carrying their own clubs for a day or two 'until the strikers have been starved out'. Not so on this occasion:

> *… the Club has acceded and the legal rate is a shilling. It was indeed hardly possible to resist, as unauthorised and premature statements by the Secretary had practically committed the Club to the change without its being consulted. Another triumph for the Labour Agitation.*

It is not clear whether Linskill had been sympathetic to the caddies' cause or whether he had simply made a gaffe.

Further on the caddie front, it was decided to hire someone to manage them. A retired policeman, Chiddington, was engaged as caddie master at 10 shillings per week during term time, working from noon until 4pm. As well as making a register of caddies he was also required to 'clear the way for players going onto the Links'.

More prosaically, at the October 1890 EGM, H M Braybrooke (Pembroke) was elected captain for the 1891 Lent term. Cecil Cancellor had resigned after two terms. He played off a handicap of 16 so perhaps he was a stopgap when Colt stepped down early? Whatever the reason, his contribution was hugely appreciated with several speeches at a club meeting in high praise of the energetic way in which he had conducted his duties.

The weather that winter was miserable. In January 1891 it was reported that there had been a 'tedious nine weeks of severe frost and intense cold' but that the golf course had not suffered as badly as other commons in Cambridge which consisted of 'vast sheets of ice'.

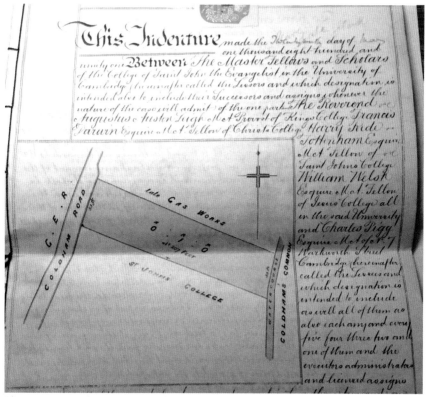

The 1891 80-year lease agreement between St John's College and the CUGC lessees for the land where the new club house would be built, about 200 yards north of the existing pavilion.

Perhaps the weather enabled the members to focus their attention more fully on the proposed new clubhouse. It was initially decided to buy the land upon which it would be sited but this proved to be prohibitively expensive. However, land belonging to St John's was identified and the college offered an 80-year lease at a rate of £40 per acre. The club anticipated requiring a quarter of an acre. The site was in a field located between Coldham Road and the border of Coldham Common. The town council granted the club's application to bridge the ditch which separated the field from the common 'and to add to security and appearance, a drawbridge is suggested'. The actual lease document resides in St John's archives, the first page of which is shown on page 61.

An initial design for the clubhouse was prepared. It was commented that 'the new Clubhouse's beauty will be in its irregularity'. It included a general club-room where members' boxes would be placed, a reading room, lavatories and dressing rooms and rooms for the professional, who would in future live in the clubhouse as its custodian. It was also decided that the existing wooden clubhouse would be moved and utilised as a workshop and drying room. It was further suggested that the design would include a raised balcony with seating 'for the idlers under the eaves, whence they can watch the various demeanours of returning golfers'.

The clubhouse was estimated to cost about £1,000 (about £120,000 in today's money). It was noted that this sum might be difficult to raise as the club is 'not so much identified with the Dons as it is at Oxford'.[37] A subscription list was opened, with the club offering to pay 4 per cent on loans over £10. By 1 December 1890, £300 had been raised.

On 16 February 1891, the usual terminal competition for the Linskill Cup and the Pirie (handicap) Medal took place in fine weather. The links were 'in capital order' as prepared by the professionals, Gourlay and Lonie. Perhaps the most notable feature of the competition was the appearance of Mr J L Low (Clare) playing off a handicap of 3, who came second and who was also elected onto the committee that same evening.

John Laing Low was a major figure in the history of CUGC. He was born in Perthshire in Scotland in 1869 and came up to Cambridge in October 1890. Apart from, in due course, becoming the captain for two years (in 1891-92 and 1892-93), he would also become the first captain of The Oxford and Cambridge Golfing Society when it was founded in 1898. He represented Scotland at golf in 1904 and was captain of the first golf team to visit America. He would go on to

---

[37] Apparently most of the money spent on the new course laid out at Headington was lent by the many Fellows who formed a large section of OUGC

become a respected writer about golf and worked on the staff of the *Pall Mall Gazette* and the *Athletic News*. He died in 1929, aged 60.

With regard to John Low's time at Cambridge, Bernard Darwin wrote, almost swooningly:

> *When he was Captain of the Cambridge Club, Coldham Common was crowded, really crowded, with players; and when it is remembered that Coldham was the most repellent of all courses, and that in the early 'nineties' very few undergraduates had ever played golf before coming up, there could be no more eloquent instance of what one man can persuade other men to do, through sheer personal attraction.*

John Low, CUGC captain 1891-92 and 1892-93.

On 23 February, the St Andrews handicap medal was played for. Reflecting the growth in members of the club, 42 competitors participated, the largest reported entry to any competition in the club's history to that point.

It was subsequently announced in April 1891 that since 1 October, 120 new members had joined CUGC. Interestingly, it was also noted that:

> *Gentlemen, not members of the 'Varsity can join the CUGC as hon. members, and many have availed themselves of this privilege.*

There was also mention of a town club being formed in Cambridge, but nothing seems to have come of it at that time.

The 1890-91 academic year was the second (after 1883-84) in which there was a different captain each term, with H M Joshua (Trinity) being elected for the Easter term. In March 1991, at the usual Wimbledon venue, Cambridge beat Oxford by the fairly convincing margin of 16 holes up to 5, and six matches to two.

Four days after the Varsity match, an interesting match took place at Coldham Common between CUGC and the 'Hon Ivo Bligh's (Old Cantabs) team'. Ivo Francis Walter Bligh would become the 8th Earl of Darnley. He was better known as a cricketer, representing Cambridge against Oxford on four occasions between 1877 and 1881. Subsequently he captained England and the MCC in the first ever Test series against Australia with The Ashes at stake in 1882-83.[38] England won the series down under and the Hon Ivo Bligh was presented with a small urn containing 'the ashes of English cricket'. Meanwhile in the 16-aside match, CUGC won 6 holes up, although A M Chance's 12 hole victory over E Lehmann was a significant factor. This match was a forerunner of the yet-to-be-formed Oxford and Cambridge Golfing Society.

1891-92

In April 1891, the amusingly initialled D A M Brown had been voted in as captain for the forthcoming Michaelmas term. Unfortunately, he 'went down', so a new election was held in October and John Low became the Captain. New members continued to flood in, with 83 joining in the Michaelmas term in 1891.

On 17 November 1891, when the Linskill Cup and Pirie Medal were played for, John Low, playing off of scratch, returned the best gross score of 86 to win the former and Claude L Barrow (Jesus) with a net 79 won the latter. The following week, 43 players competed for the St Andrews handicap medal which was won by C E Hambro. Charles Eric Hambro would go on to run the family merchant banking business, became the MP for Wimbledon and was knighted for services during the First World War.

At the club EGM that evening, a couple of interesting minutes were recorded. First, an inter-collegiate cup was mooted, to be played for by teams of five. There were clearly enough undergraduates playing golf at this time to contemplate such a competition. But, without explanation, the motion was not carried. Second, it was noted that the old roller was to be sold to the Girton Ladies Club. On further investigation, the following was discovered in a history of Girton College written in 1933.[39]

> *A Golf Club was formed in 1891, and it was a source of some pride that the Girton grounds were large enough to contain quite a good little course; but this came to an end when the new buildings of 1902 encroached on the course.*

---

[38]England having lost to Australia for the first time on home soil at the Oval in March 1882.

[39]Stephen B, *Girton College, 1869-1932*, Cambridge, 1933.

Clearly, the appetite for golf during this era was not restricted to the young gentlemen of Cambridge.

However, even in these heydays, new problems still cropped up from time to time on Coldham Common. The recently appointed President of the club, Charles Pigg, had to see the mayor about a heap of manure placed on the common by the town surveyor. And, the hon sec, Linskill, had to communicate with Mr W B Redfarn of the Cambridgeshire Volunteers regarding the deposit of rubbish on the links. This latter problem must have been resolved amicably as Redfarn was shortly thereafter made an honorary life member of the club. In February 1892, the links policeman, Chiddington, was laid up having been struck by half a brick by one of the caddies. For this the caddie received a suspension.

On 2 February 1892, the terminal competition was played on a day that was 'fine but intensely cold, and a perfect gale was blowing across the green'. Linskill reported to *The Field* that:

> Both cup and medal fell to Mr J Low (Clare), a well-known Carnoustie player, with the magnificent scratch score of 79.

It was deemed so impressive that the hole-by-hole score was also published. However, the standard of golf at Coldham was clearly on the up; no sooner had Low been lauded when E C P Boyd (Trinity) shot 76 with, as Linskill reported, 'perfect play'. He also mentioned that these low scores had been achieved on the 9-hole course but noted that:

> When the long medal round, including the Abney holes, is played, it would be marvellous nay, almost impossible to get round under 80. The long round includes two of the longest holes to be seen on any British links.

It was also reported that Mr Claude L Barrow had offered to present 'a new and handsome gold medal to be competed for under handicap in the October and Lent terms'. The Barrow Medal was played for over the next twenty years. Sadly, Claude Loraine Barrow died in June 1903 in the Paris to Madrid race when he crashed his car into a tree.

While researching this book, the author discovered that the Barrow Medal appeared at auction at Bonhams in June 2011 and was sold for £624 (including premium). The medal was purchased by Jim McCormick, an American collector of golfing memorabilia. Mr McCormick kindly provided photographs of the Barrow Medal. It is made of silver gilt in the shape of a star with an enamel centre featuring the University of Cambridge coat of arms. The wording upon it, 'Non

Sine Pulvere Palma 1892', means 'no laurel without effort' or in today's parlance, 'no pain, no gain'. On the reverse, there is the traditional golfing wording 'Far and Sure' and that it had been won by I W Heron-Maxwell in 1892. We will return to this in due course.

The Barrow Medal, obverse and reverse.

On 27 February 1892, it was reported that the new golf clubhouse would be ready at the end of the Easter vacation:

> It consists of a very large dining room surrounded with boxes, a large reading room, dressing rooms, and suitable offices, a large hall for boxes, & co., shop for professional, and a two-storey house for the head professional. It is to be lighted throughout with gas.

Apropos of this, it was also reported that since October (i.e. the beginning of the 1891/92 academic year), 131 new members had joined CUGC!

In warming up for the Varsity match, CUGC played Royal Blackheath and Great Yarmouth, two strong clubs, on two successive days at Coldham Common in late February. The results were encouraging, convincing victories by 36 holes and 46 holes respectively. On 10 March, the match against Oxford was once again played at Wimbledon Common, although there had been some discussions about moving it to St George's at Sandwich. As in 1890, there was snow on the ground and the greens were swept a small distance around each hole to make them playable. Cambridge must have been the snow specialists, because they won again, this time by 12 holes up, although two of their victories (out of three) accounted for 16 holes.

On 30 April 1892, it was reported that:

The handsome new golf clubhouse, which stands in a field adjoining the links, was formally opened on Saturday, April 23. Then Charles Pigg, the President, in a neat speech, declared the clubhouse open, and expressed pleasure at the wonderful popularity of golf in Cambridge. Speeches were also made by the captain, Mr John L Low, and the hon. sec., Mr W T Linskill. The architect is Mr B D Cancellor, Winchester, brother of the ex-Captain of the Club, and the builders Messrs Thoday and Son, Cambridge. On Saturday, the links were crowded with red-coated golfers.

On 29 April, the first competition for the Barrow Medal took place with over 40 players entering. It was decided to play the 'bogey system' of hole play rather than stroke play, off two-thirds handicap to decide the winner. The fixed score of 'the bogey man' was set at 82 for the eighteen holes. The winner was decisively Mr H Parker (Trinity Hall) playing off 6, who was 6 up; second place fell to Mr W Hartree who was 2 up. Mr I Heron-Maxwell was reported to have come third with a result of 1 down. This is curious because it is Heron-Maxwell's name that appears on the reverse side of the Barrow Medal.

On 1 May 1892, the Royston golf club was established. The course had been laid out by 'two gentlemen … from the Cambridge University Golf Club', who were in fact John L Low and William T Linskill, who both became founder members of the club. Apparently the course that they laid out followed much of the original eighteen holes set out by George Gosset and Andrew Graham Murray in 1869.[40]

1892-93

When the links at Coldham Common re-opened in October 1892, it was noted that '5 professionals are in residence'. James Gourlay was still the head professional and two of his 'St Andrews assistants' were mentioned by name, J Tabor and H Hurry. The club continued to flourish, with over 80 new members in the first month. Presumably as a consequence of the demand for golf equipment in Cambridge it was noted that 'Albert Tingey, from Tom Morris's, St Andrews, has opened a shop on the Newmarket Road, and Gray, in Rose Crescent, has also got a Scotch clubmaker'. Albert Tingey had indeed learned his trade under Old Tom Morris, and was particularly well-known for his putters, but he was actually born in nearby Newmarket in 1869 and would become the professional at Brancaster in Norfolk from 1892-99. Grays of Cambridge was founded by the rackets champion H J Gray in 1855 and still had a shop in Sidney Street, Cambridge until 2006.

[40]Allsopp H et al, *A Century of Golf, The History of Royston Golf Club*, 1892-1992, 1992

The club competitions were now extremely well-attended with regularly over 40 participants. The standard of golf was also on the rise; in the competition for the Linskill Cup and Pirie Medal on 15 November 1892, four players were recorded to be off scratch and another seven had single figure handicaps. There was also competition for the captaincy of the club, with three standing for election: J L Low, E C P Boyd and A M Chance. Low took two-thirds of the votes cast to become captain for the second time.

The second competition for the Barrow Medal took place on 29 November 1892 with the Bogey score set at 84 this time. The winner, off a handicap of 5 and 4 holes up on the bogey man, was none other than Mr Ivor Heron-Maxwell. One could imagine that Mr H Parker, the first winner, might not be best pleased if he knew that it is Mr Heron-Maxwell's name, and not his, that is etched for posterity on the reverse side of the Barrow Medal.

The prospect of the GER laying a railway line cutting through Coldham Common returned in 1892. Once again CUGC combined forces with other parties – the Coldham Commoners, the Commons Preservation Society and the Rifle Volunteers – to try to head it off. Letters of objection were again written to the town corporation.

Meanwhile the battle with the flooding of the common continued. In January 1893, the club received permission from the town clerk to once again lay drainage; this time at the so-called Abney holes at the Newmarket Road end of the common.

Cambridge took a powerful side, maybe their strongest ever, to face Oxford at Wimbledon Common on 10 March 1892. Cambridge's seventh and eighth men (H Parker and C C Bethune) played off 3 and 5 respectively; the other six were all scratch golfers. Cambridge won 32 holes up, winning 7 matches and losing 1 (by one hole). Even that solitary win for Oxford was fortuitous; with the match all square, L Robertson's 'drive to the last hole struck the wire of the plantation to the left and glanced on to the green, and the hole was all but taken in two'. The result also put Cambridge ahead in the overall series for the first time, 8 matches to 7.

1893-94

As the new academic year began, there were three professionals from St Andrews in attendance at the clubhouse, James Gourlay, Davie Gourlay and W Brown. The 18-hole course was said to be in 'capital order' and thanks to the recent draining, perfectly dry.

On 11 November 1893, an article probably by Linskill appeared in *The Field*, referring to the formation of the Worlington and Newmarket golf club. It noted that:

> *The round, which was laid out by Tom Dunn, the Tooting Bec professional, at present consists of nine holes, and is about one and a half miles in length; but a long round, containing the orthodox eighteen holes, is in course of preparation, and will be ready for play soon.*

Linskill was somewhat presumptuous. The second nine holes were deemed not to be as good as the first nine and Worlington remains a 9-hole course to this day. It was also announced that amongst the club's officers was one William T Linskill. On 17 November, Linskill brought the captain and several of the committee of CUGC to Worlington to sample the course. The establishment of Worlington would become a highly significant one in due course for the Cambridge University Golf Club.

On 23 November 1893, *The Cambridge Review* noted that 'Old Tom Morris, the GOM (Grand Old Man) of Golf, was staying at Kettering at present, and from thence proceeds to Wellingborough, to lay out a golf green; he is expected to pay a visit to Cambridge shortly'. There was no follow-up article to say whether in fact he did or not. The article also said that Andrew Kirkaldy from St Andrews, who was the professional at Royston at that time, was expected at Coldham during the term. 'Andra', as he was known, was one of the great characters in golf from that era. He never won the Open Championship, although he finished in the top ten on 14 occasions, including losing in a play-off to Willie Park Jr in 1889. Unfortunately, he left Royston to return to St Andrews before he could test his golf at Coldham Common.

In the first two months of the new golfing year, 65 new members had joined. Getting from their colleges to the golf links was fairly straightforward – new members were reminded that the East Road (horse-drawn) tram could be taken from the Senate House to within a four-minute walk from the club. The tram service had begun in 1880. The tramway consisted of a 6-inch (0.15m) deep concrete bed upon which wooden sleepers were laid with steel girder rails attached to the wooden sleepers. The registered offices, stables and tram shed were located at 184 East Road, where the Tram Depot pub is located today. The figure below illustrates the popularity of the trams until eventually they were superseded by motor buses in the early 1900s.

Senate House to East Road horse-drawn tram service.

A change took place to the terminal competitions in Michaelmas 1893. While the Linskill Cup remained as the main scratch prize, it was decided to split the field for the handicap prize; the St Andrews Medal to be awarded for the best net score for the golfer with a handicap of 15 and below, and the Pirie prize to go to the best net score for the golfer with a handicap of 16 and above. The winner of the St Andrews Medal would henceforth receive a small replica. And, the Pirie Medal would be 'abolished, and its place to be taken by a Memento' which would be given to the winner to keep on each occasion.

Nothing more is said in the club's minutes about the original Pirie Medal, which was the first trophy played for in the club in 1876, donated by the first captain, Rev George Pirie. To this day its whereabouts are unknown.

At the beginning of the Lent term, 18 January 1894, it was announced in *The Cambridge Review* that:

> *The GER line over the Common is not to be commenced yet awhile, and the Rifle Butts are not to be removed till March, so golfers will be able to play the present course all this term. When the railway is finished and the Butts moved, the course will have to be laid out afresh.*

It is not recorded in the CUGC minutes whether the club went down without a fight or not. Ultimately, the expansion of the town and the need to build housing (for railway workers) must have won the day. So, unlike in 1887, the GER got its way. If Coldham Common was already a poor example of a golf links, it was only about to get worse.

Meanwhile, the club had a busy schedule of matches in the term ahead: Old Cantabs, Stevenage, North Beds, Royston, Notts, Royal Blackheath, Great Yarmouth and an Army match were all slated in advance of the Varsity match.

There were 39 participants on the terminal competition day on 13 February 1894. And, there was a surprise winner of the Linskill Cup – Linskill himself, by a margin of 4 shots. There must have been a change in the club rules to allow this to happen because for many years the Linskill Cup was only open to undergraduates. In the CUGC Minutes it is noted (by Linskill) that he would prefer not to take the Cup and begged for the three players, Le Fleming, Upcher and Johnston, who had tied for second place to play off for its possession. It is not recorded whether this took place or not although on 22 April it is noted in the minutes that Mr Upcher stated that the Cup case with the names thereon was missing.

When the Varsity match came round on 3 March 1894, for the first time it was not played at Wimbledon. There had been agitations for a few years, more so from Oxford, to move the match to a seaside links, of which St George's at Sandwich was favoured. Linskill and Cambridge had always preferred Wimbledon primarily due to convenience in terms of travel (for both sides). Interestingly, John Low played for Cambridge in the top match, despite the fact that he had gone down the previous year. However, the rules allowed a player to represent his University up to four times and no more than once after he had graduated. Hence, Low's appearance. Although he won his match (1 up against R B Pearson), overall Cambridge no longer had the depth that they had in their wonderful side of the previous year and lost by 13 holes.

As the academic year drew to a close, it was noted in the minutes that the club remained overdrawn by the same amount as in the previous year (£293). It was also noted that subscriptions for the year had amounted to £352 and that it was proposed to raise the annual subscription for all new members in the forthcoming year from 30 shillings (£1.50) to £2. This infers that in 1993-94, CUGC would have had 235 paying members.

1894-95

As the new academic year began in October 1894, once again there were three professionals in attendance at Coldham – the two Gourlays, James and Davie, as in the previous year, but W Brown had been appointed the head professional at Cardiff golf club and he was replaced by Willie Duncan, an apprentice of Old Tom Morris, who had, like several others before him, come down from St Andrews.

Linskill was required to write to *The Cambridge Review* to dispel the rumour that the links were flooded. In any case, more members were pouring in – over 60 had joined by mid-November and as Linskill put it, 'and the cry is, still they come'. One in particular who came, and who was in fact the first to be elected that year as noted in the minute book, was Bernard Darwin of whom Linskill said 'is miles away the best'.

As mentioned earlier, his father was Frank Darwin who was President of CUGC from 1889-91 and his grandfather was Charles Darwin. But Bernard was not inclined to follow them along the evolutionary path. He was very keen on sports and learned to play golf around the age of 8 playing at Aberdovey where his mother's family came from, as well as on Coldham Common.[41] He came up from Eton to Trinity College in October 1894. Like Low before him, Darwin played in three Varsity matches; he also captained the club in 1897. He subsequently moved to London to start his career in the legal profession but golf was such a draw that when he was offered the opportunity to write about it for *The Evening Standard* and *Country Life* he dropped law and became a journalist. He also became

'The Golf Correspondent' for *The Times*. He played for England on numerous occasions, reached the semi-final of the Amateur Championship twice and played in the first Walker Cup in America.[42] He was a member of many golf clubs, although Woking and Rye were probably the ones closest to his heart, and he was Captain of the R&A in 1934. Simply put, he was steeped in golf from childhood until his death in 1961, aged 85.

Bernard Darwin.

[41]He lived with his father and step-mother (his own mother died only a few days after he was born) at Wychfield House on the Huntingdon Road, where 'a colony of Darwins' lived. This is now part of Trinity Hall College.
[42]He was not originally selected but was there to cover the match for *The Times*. However, when the GB&I captain fell ill, Darwin was asked to step in and take his place. He lost his foursomes match but won his singles match.

Difficulties were arising once again with the caddies. It was reported in *The Cambridge Review* on 25 October 1894 that:

> *It is to be regretted that the caddies make themselves so disagreeable, but players should decline to give them a single copper for getting their balls out of the ditches. It is the duty of their own caddies to do this. The caddies who hang about the ditches are chiefly small boys. Members should be careful to engage their caddies through Chiddenton, the links policeman, who will pick out for them the best and most civil caddies.*

About a month later, Linskill reported that 'I hear no complaints whatever of the Caddies now, and Perry, the new Links Policeman, seems to have them well in hand'. Perhaps Chiddenton had become less effective after being hit by half a brick.

In early December, a famous amateur golfer visited Coldham Common – Mr F G Tait played in a foursome with Linskill and two other CUGC members. Freddie Tait, as he was more widely known, would go on to win the Amateur Championship twice, in 1896 and 1898. He also came third in the Open Championship on two occasions and was a prodigious striker of a golf ball. At St Andrews on 11 January 1893, he hit the ball 250 yards through the air; it then rolled on frozen ground and came to rest 341 yards from the tee – a world record at the time. Interestingly, his father, Peter Guthrie Tait, who was a Peterhouse undergraduate and mathematician and became the Professor of Natural Philosophy at Edinburgh University, had, in 1890, predicted from theory that the furthest a golf ball could fly was 190 yards! There was great sadness throughout the golfing world when Freddie Tait was killed while fighting in the Boer War in 1900.

Apropos of nothing, Linskill reported to *The Cambridge Review* (6 December 1894) that 'Mr Balls of Petty Cury, has kindly presented me with a handsome Golf Tobacco Jar, on which are the arms of the Royal and Ancient Golf Club of St Andrews; golfers should go and see them'. Perhaps Linskill was a much valued customer?

On 15 November 1894, the honorary secretary reported that the town clerk had informed him that in three months' time the GER would commence with its railway line across Coldham Common. Linskill remarked that the course would need to be considerably altered and he advised that the medals and matches had better be played before then. And so, on Valentine's Day, 14 February 1895, the GER line at Coldham Common was opened. The rifle butts had been moved and it was reported in *The Cambridge Independent Press* that the GER had paid the corporation the sizeable sum of £1,500 to do this. Since CUGC paid nothing to use the common to play golf, it received no payment to alter the course.

An important announcement was made in *The Cambridge Review* in November 1894:

> *The authorities of the Worlington and Newmarket Golf Club have issued a notice to the effect that 'Undergraduates of the University of Cambridge may become temporary members of the Golf Club, Worlington, with the approval of the Council, on payment in advance of a subscription of 10s. 6d. a term ....'*
> *This should prove a great boon to 'Varsity golfers, as Worlington is on sandy soil, is open all the year, and is far away the best inland green in the neighbourhood.*

Linskill's connections with Worlington must have played a role in establishing this arrangement. It was the precursor to the long term relationship which would ultimately emerge between CUGC and Royal Worlington and Newmarket Golf Club (as it became in July 1895).

In December, Gourlay handed in his notice and Willie Duncan was offered and accepted the position of head professional. His pay and conditions were reported in the minutes – £1 per week between 1 Oct and 12 May with the cottage rent-free as well as coals and gas free of charge.[43] In addition, his wife would receive in total £6 annually for cleaning the clubhouse and cooking. It was also minuted that the second professional received 15 shillings per week in term time only (and no lodgings) while the Links policeman was paid 10 shillings per week on the same basis.

The Lent term in 1895 was one of the coldest in memory. Darwin recalled it was 'the year of the long frost when people could skate all the way to Ely'. For nearly the entire Lent term, from the end of January and on into March, the course was snow-bound and as hard as ice. Darwin said that the competition for the Linskill Cup was continually postponed in the hope of kinder weather. In the end, it was decreed to play it on a snow-covered Coldham Common with small spaces cleared around each hole. In order to find their golf balls in the white landscape they used red ones. Of the occasion, Darwin wrote:

> *I remember clearly only one stroke – my first. The first hole was a one-shotter and being wholly out of practice, as we all were, I came very near to missing the globe. I said I had slipped; perhaps I really had; at any rate the ball, in the words of the rule, left its position and came to rest in another place, not very far off. I was thankful to get a five. I must have played better afterwards, for my score was 92.*

---

[43]In all likelihood, the professional would return to Scotland in the summer months to seek employment as a greenkeeper or caddie, or play in money matches to make a living.

It was good enough to win by several strokes. Later in life, Darwin wondered whether he might be one of the few people still alive to have won a scratch medal with a red ball.

On 1 March 1895, it was reported in *The Cambridge Independent Press* that:

> *Alfred Browne of Coldham Lane was charged with stealing a golf ball valued*
> *at 9d. from a ditch in Coldham Common, the property of Mr Robert Leveson*
> *on 26th inst. John Perry, gatekeeper at the Golf Ground saw the defendant*
> *get the ball that had been knocked into a ditch and covered it in mud.*
> *The defendant was bound over in the sum of £5 and his father in £5 to come*
> *up for judgement if called upon within the next three months.*

Doubtless Alfred's father would not have been best pleased.

The Varsity match on 20 March 1895, again at Sandwich, was a tight affair with Cambridge sneaking home by 11 holes to 8. Darwin won his match. He also, in his first year, won the Linskill Cup on each of the three occasions it was played.

1895-96

When the Michaelmas term began, Willie Duncan was still the head professional. The re-constructed 18-hole course (due to the GER line) was deemed to be a great improvement on the old round. And, hot and cold luncheon was now available at the clubhouse. Even more dramatic news was the announcement by Linskill that he would be resigning from the post of honorary secretary as he was planning to leave Cambridge permanently at the end of the academic year and re-locate, with his family, to St Andrews.

On the terminal competition day in November 1895, Darwin won the Linskill Cup again, with a score of 76. His net 76 was also good enough to win the St Andrews Medal; the Pirie Memento was won by H M Wood (100 – 16 = net 84). Fifty-five golfers participated, the largest field ever for a CUGC competition, on that rare thing, it would seem, at Coldham Common, 'a fine day'.

Willie Duncan shot a low score of 73 around the new 18-hole course and a 'home and home' 72-hole match was arranged with Jack White of Royal Worlington and Newmarket. The first leg of 36 holes was played at Coldham Common on 25 January 1896 after which White led by three holes. The second leg was played at Worlington a week later. While 'Duncan's driving was magnificent, White holed every possible and many seemingly impossible putts'. White won by 8 and 7 overall. Jack White, who was originally from North Berwick, would go on to become the first professional at Sunningdale in 1901 and win the Open Championship at Royal St George's in 1904.

In January 1896 it was noted in the minutes that 'a ball drawn into the new railway line [was] to be taken out a club length from the railings and dropped'. There was no mention of whether there would be a penalty for doing so.

In late February, it was reported that, for the forthcoming Varsity match on 10 March, seven players had been selected by the captain (Kenneth McLean Marshall) and the secretary (Linskill) and that four players would compete for the eighth place – J G McCall (Christ's), D S Murray (Pembroke), B C Thompson (Pembroke) and H H Marriot (Clare). In the end, none of these four were selected and B Hillyard (Clare) got the eighth spot.

After two years at Sandwich, the Varsity match returned to Wimbledon Common for what turned out to be the most exciting and close-run affair to date. Three of the matches were halved and three were won one up. When Lushington (Balliol) beat Leathart (Clare) by two holes, it put Oxford three up with just the eighth match to finish. However, the late pick, Hillyard, had been a wise choice for he won three up (and just failed to win four up), so the result was a tie for the first time.

The photograph shows the Cambridge eight-man team in 1896 together with the honorary secretary, W T Linskill, dressed in high collar, knickerbockers and spats. A very youthful looking Bernard Darwin is seated on Linskill's right, while the captain, Kenneth McLean Marshall, is standing centrally within the group. The team members are resplendent in their red coats with light blue collars.

The Cambridge team and W T Linskill, 1896.

The 18-hole course at Coldham Common

The 18-hole course was first reported to have been used for the Linskill Cup in November 1887. This was not long after the map showing the 9-hole course was prepared in connection with the proposed GER railway line at that time.

Unlike the 9-hole course, no map has been uncovered showing the 18-hole layout (either pre- or post-GER line). However, one valuable piece of information was discovered in the CUGC minute book – the names and yardages of each of the eighteen holes as measured in February 1891 (i.e. before the course was altered due to the GER line). These were:

Hole	Name	Yards
1	The Road	236
2	The Magazine	281
3	The Hut	360
4	The Gas Tank	332
5	Eastward Ho!	328
6	Duffer's Ditch	282
7	The Range	332
8	Teversham Ditch	245
9	The Hedge	212
OUT		**2608**
10	The Hole Across	200
11	The Valley	253
12	The Burn	226
13	The Chimneys	257
14	The Short Hole	200
15	The Bridge	209
16	The Abney Hole	316
17	The Quarry	381
18	The Home	378
IN		**2420**
TOTAL		**5028**

The course measured just over 5,000 yards, or nearly three miles in length. *The Golfing Annual* in 1887, which provided a directory of all known golf clubs at that time, contained the following lyrical prose describing the Coldham Common course, presumably from the hand of Linskill:

> *The drainage of the Common, and sanding and sowing of the greens, have greatly improved the links. There are no very short holes. The ground is undulating, and the hazards [are] a road, several footpaths, dry ditches, two running burns and bushes & co.*

Darwin, who played there from 1894-97, wrote that:

> *This is a comparatively attractive picture, but not, I fear, a true one. Certainly there were no very short holes. They were nearly all of the same length, namely that of a drive and a pitch and nothing to pitch over.*

The names of the holes give some clues as to the layout of the course. The location of the first three holes was indicated in a report to *The Cambridge Review* in April 1990:

> *All the ground (now a perfect lake) where the first three holes, of the eighteen hole course, lie is being thoroughly and deeply drained from the rifle range railings to the road.*

So, it can be concluded that they must have been on the south side of the rifle range. The Road Hole (1st) would probably have started in the vicinity of the clubhouse with a green near Coldham's Lane, the only road abutting the common. The 2nd hole was called The Magazine. Interestingly, on the 1887 map of Coldham Common (page 53), a Magazine, presumably to store ammunition for the Rifle Range, is shown. So, the 2nd green was probably near it. The 3rd hole, The Hut, was presumably named after the rifle range Pavilion, also shown on the 1887 map.

The 4th hole was called The Gas Tank. Some writers in the past have thought that the name of this hole might have been related to a comment made by Darwin about 'a particularly pungent smell':

> *… [from a] factory, supposed by us, to be devoted to the boiling down of deceased horses into glue, which, with the wind in a certain quarter, cast its sickly trail over the Common.*

No references have shown up regarding a glue factory in the vicinity of Coldham Common at that time, however there were a number of brick and tile works nearby as well as a sewage pumping station, so maybe they accounted for the odours. The hole, however, was actually named because there was a deep muddy pond located in its vicinity which was once used as a gas tank, presumably from the days when coprolite digging took place on the common.

It is also possible to obtain a reasonably good fix on the closing four holes, the 15th to 18th. We have already made mention of the so-called 'Abney holes' which were on the narrow strip of land at the Newmarket Road end of the common. L E G Abney was on the CUGC committee in 1888-89, so presumably the holes in this area were at his suggestion. The names would suggest that the 16th, The Abney Hole, and the 17th, The Quarry (near the brick quarry) ran up and back along this finger of the common. It was also a problematic part of the common in terms of waterlogging due to the nearby brook on one side and (sometimes blocked) ditches or drains on the other. The Bridge hole, the 15th, was presumably played from the heart of the Common to a green near the bridge that connected the footpath crossing the ditch to where the Abney Hole was. The 18th Home hole would simply work its way back from the Abney holes to a green close to the clubhouse.

As best as can be made out, the remaining ten holes, from the 5th to the 14th, must have worked their way around the common in an anti-clockwise direction. The 7th hole, The Range, presumably ran parallel with the rifle range. The 8th and 9th holes, Teversham Ditch and the Hedge Hole would have been in the vicinity of the two ditches at the east end of the common where a footpath to Teversham is marked on the 1887 map. The 10th, the Hole Across, mimics the names of the St Andrews 5th and 13th holes, Hole O'Cross (out) and Hole O'Cross (in). It suggests that this hole might have cut across the common from near the boundary to create space for the following four holes, the 11th to 14th, which would have followed the northern boundary as defined by Coldham's Brook.

This was the course in 1891. The intervention of the railway line and the re-laying of the rifle range and butts in 1895 altered the course but probably the general anti-clockwise flow of the holes around the common remained. If anything, it probably shortened some of the longer holes as the course would have to be compressed into a smaller area. But, as Darwin noted:

> *...holes mattered less at Coldham than on most courses. It was perfectly flat, and you might make a hole more or less anywhere without producing any noticeable change.*

Based on this interpretation, a schematic representation of the 18-hole layout has been produced by the author and is shown against the backdrop of an aerial image of Coldham Common from 1945.

Likely layout of 18-hole course at Coldham Common in early 1890s.

7
W T Linskill
– the man and his legacy

Linskill left Cambridge at the end of the May term in 1896. He would return again for the CUGC match against Old Cantabs at Coldham Common on 27 February 1897. Although he did not play in the match, which was in itself rather surprising, it was noted that:

> *During luncheon on the day of the match ... Mr W T Linskill was presented with a silver inkstand and a pair of silver candlesticks, subscribed for by past and present members of the CUGC, in recognition of his services as Honorary Secretary from the foundation of the club in 1875 till his departure from Cambridge in 1896.*

While he was rightly lauded then, and should still be to this day, for the enormous contribution that he had made in his two decades of involvement with the Cambridge University Golf Club, it is also right and proper to stand back and try to assess his legacy more clearly. But first, let us take a closer look at who he was before we consider what he achieved.

The scholar and the gentleman

To recap, he arrived in Cambridge, with his parents William and Francis Linskill, in 1873. They bought 3 Belvoir Terrace where his parents lived for the rest of their lives. Linskill was eighteen at the time. Clearly the intention of his parents was for their son to go to the University. According to the University records, he was 'Admitted as a Pensioner' (i.e. without a scholarship or financial support) to Jesus College on 1 October 1876 but that he did not matriculate (i.e. be formally admitted to the University) until the Lent term in 1877.

How long he remained *in statu pupillari* is unclear. He first became captain of CUGC in October 1876 and (with the exception of the Easter term in 1877) he remained as captain (until E F Chance was elected in January 1884) for a period of just over seven years. He also represented Cambridge in four Varsity golf matches, the first one in 1878, then in 1879, 1882 and 1883. On each occasion, Jesus was denoted as his college. Writing in 1940, Bernard Darwin, looking back affectionately on Linskill, wrote:

> *He continued to play in the match, with a fine disregard for four-year rules, until 1883. Whether he was then still a member of his college I should doubt, for he never passed his little-go.*[44]

The 'Little-Go', or more formally the Previous Examination, typically taken in the first year of study, was intended to establish whether the student had a basic aptitude in mathematics and the classics. This was taken in advance of proceeding to the General exam for a 'pass' degree and finally the Tripos exam to obtain an Honours degree.

On investigation of the records held on Linskill at Jesus, there are no results recorded for any of these exams. The college archivist described this as 'unusual' and suggested not only that he did not graduate but that he may not have been at the college for very long at all.

Linskill was not alone in not obtaining a degree from Cambridge at that time. During the era whilst he was at Jesus, more than a third of the undergraduates left Cambridge without a degree.[45] Sporting prowess at the college attracted more attention than academic distinction. Also, sporting, dining, social and debating clubs as well as college 'traditions' were central to the experience of being there. Hence, the role of the college was, in large part, that of a finishing school for young gentlemen.

Linskill, as an only child with wealthy elderly parents, who seemed content to support him, most certainly fell into that category. With no need for him to seek employment, he would have looked forward to a life of leisure as a gentleman of the era. The pattern of his life was now becoming well-established. He would be in Cambridge for the academic year, from October to mid-May, and then he would spend the summer months in St Andrews. Whether in Cambridge or St Andrews, with the exception of Sundays, he would be on the golf links virtually every day.

---

[44]Darwin B, *Life is Sweet, Brother*, London, 1940
[45]Only a quarter of those who graduated took an honours degree; the others obtaining a 'pass' degree, www.jesus.cam.ac.uk

A lucky escape

There must have been some exceptions to this pattern because of an intriguing tale that Linskill related on a number of occasions throughout his life. He was in Scotland in December 1879 – quite specifically on 28 December. A number of variations of the story have been recorded, but the central theme has remained largely consistent.

On that day, Linskill was travelling from Edinburgh on the Dundee train to get to St Andrews. The train journey was complicated. A first train took him from Edinburgh to Granton. The passengers then crossed the Firth of Forth by ferry to Burntisland on the Fife coast and boarded a second train to travel onwards to Dundee. Because it was a Sunday, there were no trains operating on the branch line to St Andrews, so Linskill had arranged a coach to go from St Andrews to collect him at Leuchars. It was a very stormy night and the journey took much longer than usual. The train eventually pulled into Leuchars at around 7pm. Linskill disembarked but there was no coach to be seen. Concerned that he could be stuck there, he decided to re-board the train and go on to Dundee to stay there for the night. However, just as the train was departing, a station porter spotted his coach arriving, got the train to stop, allowing Linskill to disembark and get to St Andrews that night after all. He was not to know at the time, but 15 minutes later and only 8 miles further on as the train was crossing the Tay at the height of the storm, the bridge collapsed taking the train with it. There were no survivors. In all, 75 lives were lost in what is still known to this day as the Tay Bridge disaster. Linskill was twenty-four at the time and as a consequence of this very lucky escape would go on to live another 50 years.

There is one curious variation to the above story. When Linskill related the tale to H V Morton, the journalist and pioneering travel writer, near the end of his life, he said that he was coming up from Edinburgh with a friend.[46] In a more recent book written by Robin Lumley he related that Linskill was travelling with a young boy 'whose identity and relationship with Linskill is unknown' and that he carried the boy off the train to the coach when it arrived.[47]

[46]Morton H V, *In Search of Scotland*, H V Morton, London, 1929
[47]Lumley R, *The Tay Bridge Disaster: the People's Story*, Stroud, 2013

In researching this aspect of the story, this author came across an autobiography titled, *A Pelican's Tale*, written in 1919 by Frank M Boyd. Within it there appears the following passage:

> *Before departing to [Germany] something happened which nearly rendered the idea of going there or anywhere else futile … I had gone over to Edinburgh from St Andrews to see the pantomime … I was to have returned on Saturday from Edinburgh, but a great storm arose and the boat could not cross the Forth … I found that a train would leave Edinburgh for Granton in the [Sunday] evening, and it was hoped that a crossing to Burntisland might be effected …. That night it took two and a half hours, and at last, we got into harbour at Burntisland, and there the Dundee train was waiting ….. I had to get out at a small junction station called Leuchars on my way to St Andrews … It was well that I did get out there, for the train and its passengers never reached their destination … not a soul was saved from the terrible Tay Bridge disaster.*

Frank Mortimer Boyd was born in February 1863 and so would have been sixteen at the time of the disaster. The uncanny similarity of the two recollections means that he must have been the boy who had travelled with and been carried off the train by Linskill. Frank Boyd, it transpires, was the son of Reverend A K H Boyd, the minister of the Holy Trinity Church in St Andrews. Reverend Boyd was an extremely well-known figure in the town (and more widely) and would go on to become the Moderator of the General Assembly of the Church of Scotland in 1890. It would seem that Linskill had taken Frank Boyd to Edinburgh to see some theatrical shows for a few days perhaps as a Christmas treat.

Boyd's autobiography was called '*The Pelican's Tale*' because he set up a newspaper in London in 1889 called The Pelican. Apparently it was a paper for 'the man about town', specialising in sporting journalism, clubs, theatre and London life. In the 1890s, Boyd took Linskill on as a correspondent reporting from Cambridge.[48] It suggests that a bond had been formed between the two men arising out of their near-death experience in 1879. Darwin wrote:

> *[Linskill] was for a while the Cambridge correspondent for a paper called The Pelican, edited by Mr Frank Boyd, who was one of the great St Andrews family. The readers of that rather scandalous journal must have gained the impression that there were only two places in Cambridge, Coldham Common and the Theatre Royal.*

---

[48]One further connection existed between the Boyd family and Linskill. H B Boyd, another of A K H Boyd's sons, was captain of CUGC in 1886/87 and played in three Varsity matches.

We cannot say what impact this traumatic event had on Linskill's attitude to life thereafter. Gentlemen of the Victorian era were not likely to bare their souls in public about such matters. Perhaps, Linskill's re-telling of the story throughout his life was his way of acknowledging how lucky he felt he was to have survived. Maybe it roused him to live each day to the full. He certainly did that for the rest of his days.

Other aspects of Linskill's life

The regular pattern that Linskill had established in his life in Cambridge was subject to one significant change in 1881 – he got married. William Thomas Linskill wed Jessie Munro Stewart, the daughter of James Stewart, in Edinburgh on 7 March 1881. He was twenty-five at the time. We do not know where they met or anything about how romance between them blossomed but it would be a reasonable guess to suggest that it was in the summer months in St Andrews when the town was inundated with visitors.

There soon followed children. William and Jessie Linskill had three daughters: Violet Frances was born on 30 December 1881; Mary Seton was born in March 1883, but sadly died 6 months later; and Nora Douglas was born on 6 November 1886.[49] By this time, he had moved out of his parent's home; he was recorded to have been living at 48 New Square in Cambridge in 1884.

Even with a growing family, Linskill maintained his regular outings on the links at Coldham Common. But, it was not just golf – he had other strings to his bow. Darwin noted that his other interests included 'theatricals, high church ritual and, when he lived at St Andrews, antiquarian research into that city's historic ruins, a subject on which he was, I believe, very learned'.[50] Perhaps alluding to Linskill's somewhat eccentric character, he remarked that 'probably no-one else has combined so extensive and peculiar a knowledge of such divergent subjects'.

The tonal qualities of Linskill's voice are well-documented and made him well-suited to the theatre. Darwin spoke of his:

> … *tremendous voice which boomed and thundered across that flat expanse [of Coldham Common], and a gift of picturesque language never excelled. Tangled ingenuities of profanity poured forth in a magnificent stream.*

---

[49]Nora died in 1949 (age 63) and Violet died in 1957 (age 76). Neither married. They are buried together with their father and mother in the Western Cemetery in St Andrews. The infant Mary is buried with her grandparents in Mill Road Cemetery in Cambridge.
[50]We will turn to his antiquarian interests in St Andrews in Chapter 10 when we examine the later years of his life spent there.

H V Morton commented that, even towards the end of his life, he had 'an enormous voice' and that:

> *Mr Linskill has a trick of clearing his voice and booming the word 'however', which has the effect of a wet rag wiped over a blackboard, clearing it for the next topic.*

That voice was obviously put to good use in the theatre. According to Darwin, Linskill's preference seemed to be for musical comedy. He had befriended a Mr Redfarn who had started an amateur dramatics club, 'The Bijou', around 1875. This was the same W T Redfarn who became Mayor of Cambridge on four occasions in the 1880s and who had received honorary membership of CUGC in 1891. Redfarn would go on to open the New Theatre on St Andrews Street in 1896, about the time that Linskill left for St Andrews for good.

In *Thomas Hodge, the golf artist of St Andrews*, the author Harry Langton, included a chapter titled, 'The Eccentrics', of which there were but two and one of them was Linskill. He wrote:

> *He claimed to have toured Britain for nine years with an opera company …*
> *He used his foghorn voice to staggering effect, singing musical hall songs he had composed himself. His favourite was entitled 'Have you ever seen an oyster walk upstairs?'*

As to his high church proclivities, Darwin wrote that there was one story about Linskill that he hoped was true. Apparently he was seen walking down Trinity Street smoking a pipe with evident relish and carrying on his shoulder a large golden cross. A friend who met him suggested that this was rather irreverent to which Linskill replied perfectly seriously, 'It's alright, the thing isn't consecrated yet.' In Darwin's view this was absolutely in character:

> *He knew the rules, as he did the golfing ones, and was a stickler for them;*
> *if it had been consecrated, he would have treated the emblem with the*
> *utmost reverence.*

You would probably not forget Linskill if you met him. It was not just his voice and his eclectic interests that made him distinctive, there was also how he looked. Again Darwin provides the description:

> *His appearance was striking, at once fierce and indefinably humorous, with long, drooping, curly moustaches, a nose not wholly noble, and one unvarying knickerbocker suit, a very tall collar and very tall spats, well adapted to the Coldham mud.*

This description is supported by the photograph earlier showing Linskill posing with the Cambridge team from 1896. Thomas Hodge, who produced numerous portraits and caricatures of the great and good members of the R&A, captured Linskill at lunch eating 'Mince collops [meat balls] – between the rounds'.

Portrait of W T Linskill from *Thomas Hodge, the golf artist of St Andrews* by Harry Langton, 2000.

Linskill the golfer

Since Linskill played so much golf, it is curious to speculate how good he was. In all competitions that he played in at Coldham Common he played off scratch and there were certainly times when he was an equal amongst the best undergraduates in the club.

His Varsity match record was not so good. In the very first match in 1878, he lost 12 holes down (having been 9 down after 9) to W S W Wilson, Oxford's third string behind Horace Hutchinson and Andy Stewart, two of the very best golfers of that era. In 1879, he did a great deal better, only losing by 1 hole to Andy Stuart.

Indeed as commented earlier, Horace Hutchinson remarked that it would have been a huge upset if Linskill had won, for at St Andrews Stuart might be expected to give Linskill as many as 9 shots in an 18-hole match. Linskill did not play in 1880 due to injury and the 1881 match was cancelled due to the awful weather that year. In 1882, he returned to the side but lost by 4 holes to Sir Ludovic James Grant, a Scot who would go on to become the Professor of Law at Edinburgh University. In his fourth and final outing in 1883, Linskill played Sir Ludovic again, this time in the top match, and managed his best result – a half. In the major R&A competitions of that era, he fared no better, his name never appearing on any of the winners' lists.

Charles Blair Macdonald, the great pioneer of American golf, who knew Linskill when they were both in St Andrews in the early 1870s noted:

> *William T Linskill has been a conspicuous figure in golf more owing to his devotion than to his pre-eminence as a player in the game, though he was a fine foursomes partner.*

His swing was commented upon by none other than Horace Hutchinson in his famous book, *Golf*, from the *Badminton Library Series* in 1890. This appeared in a chapter on differing golf styles:

> *The 'Double-jointed' is a style which really does require [a] peculiar physical conformation for its exhibition in highest perfection … Its individuality consists in a tremendously exaggerated length of backswing – so much so that Mr W T Linskill, perhaps its chief exponent, is said to have sometimes knocked his ball from off the tee with the club-head as it swung round until it became quite vertical again behind his back.*

However, Linskill did excel in one area, putting. Again, from Horace Hutchinson:

> *The best putters we have seen used their wrists greatly – Jamie Allan, in his best days, Mr A F Macfie and Mr W T Linskill, are names that, among a host of fine putters, occur to us. All these players putted almost exclusively with the wrist and let the club swing very far through after the ball."*

This was exalted company indeed. Jamie Allan, a professional, came second in the Open Championship in 1879 and Allan Macfie won the first Amateur Championship (beating Hutchinson into second place) in 1885.

Darwin called Linskill a putting genius, especially at Coldham Common 'on those greens of beaten mud, which at their best rather resembled a head of hair plastered down with brilliantine'. He recalled the occasion when someone suggested to Linskill that a putter was not the proper implement for putting on those greens:

> *His voice rang out like a trumpet, "By gad," he cried, or words to that effect, "I can bang them down," and taking his wooden putter he did bang them down from all quarters of the green; but then he was one of the great putters with a freedom of wrist that I have never since seen equalled.*

Perhaps rather surprisingly, given the overall standard of his golf, Linskill wrote a book on how to play, called *Golf*. It was part of the *All-England Series* on how to play a variety of sports and was published by George Bell & Sons in 1889. It must have sold reasonably well as a second edition was published in 1892. This should also be put into a broader context. Horace Hutchinson's seminal book of instruction, *Hints on the Game of Golf* had only come out a few years before, in 1886, followed by Sir Walter Simpson's book, *The Art of Golf in 1887*. Linskill's book was essentially an introduction to golf consisting of only 54 pages. In a Prefatory Note, he says:

> *In writing this little treatise on Golf, I have endeavoured to maintain brevity and conciseness. Doubtless in regard to the first of these qualifications I have succeeded; but in the matter of conciseness, if there be any part of the subject on which a beginner would like any further explanation, or any further information, I should at any time be only too glad to answer him by letter.*

If only all authors were so very kind. Given his talent for putting, it is interesting to read what he had to say:

> *Aim at the back of the hole … and allow the putter, in its motion, to follow the ball.*

Still good advice to this day.

Linskill's legacy

There are three things for which Linskill should undoubtedly be remembered and revered for in the annals of the Cambridge University Golf Club – his endeavour in creating a golf course at Coldham Common and with it the formation of the club there; his initiative in getting the Varsity match started when golf at both universities was still in its infancy; and the central role he played over twenty years in taking CUGC from modest beginnings to become a substantial and well-respected club. These are not without caveats and, furthermore, we should not invest too much in the idea that Linskill was a deep thinker or a grand strategist. If all of this had a purpose, it was simply to enable him to do what he enjoyed doing most and that was to play, in convivial company, as much golf as he could.

First, let's consider the formation of the club at Coldham Common. There were others involved too, not least Alexander Doleman and Reverend George Pirie, but it was Linskill who put in the hard yards. He 'discovered' Coldham Common. In the early days he mowed the greens and cut holes, and he encouraged newcomers to take up this relatively unknown game. And, he did all of this at the age of 20, even before he had been admitted to the University. His enthusiasm for golf and his extrovert personality drew others in. He attracted sufficient numbers to get the club up and running and to make it sustainable in what was inevitably a transient community of Cambridge undergraduates coming up and going down.

While all of this should be lauded, it is necessary to rectify one commonly reported misconception, that Linskill founded the Cambridge University Golf Club in 1875. Two sources of evidence call this date into question.

Linskill himself wrote to *The Field* in January 1876 saying, 'Is it not a pity that a regular club cannot be formed here, as it is (I believe) at the sister university?'. The first official evidence of the existence of the Linskill-inspired Cambridge Golf Club appears in *The Field* in an article dated 18 March 1876 announcing the forthcoming '*Cambridge Golf Club Prize Meeting*' on 22 March. No evidence has been unearthed to date the club any earlier.

Why did he persist with 1875? Perhaps he blurred the distinction between 'getting golf started' and 'the formation of a club'. Maybe there was also a bit of partisanship on his part. In that regard he has been successful; it remains frequently stated to this day that golf got underway at both Oxford and Cambridge in the same year, 1875.

The second and more substantive reason why Linskill's statement should not be accepted is that a Cambridge University Golf Club had already existed at an earlier date, in 1869. It had seventeen paid up members, an honorary secretary (Claude Carnegie) and a captain (George Gosset) and remained functional until all had gone down by 1871. So, the Linskill-inspired CUGC was a re-formation rather than a formation. Other golf clubs and golfing societies have gone through similar ups and downs in terms of activity throughout their histories. The two oldest clubs in England, Blackheath and Old Manchester, are cases in point, yet it is still accepted that Blackheath as an institution can be dated back to 1766 and Old Manchester to 1818.

We must assume that Linskill did not know of the earlier club when he was involved in its re-establishment in 1876. However, it remains rather surprising that he did not subsequently acknowledge its existence as the three principal figures from 1869 were almost certainly known to him.

The captain, George Gosset, one of the Gossets of Royal North Devon fame, was an extremely well-known golfer. He won numerous competitions at Westward Ho! as well as at Wimbledon (where he was a member of the London Scottish Club) and at Hoylake. These were all extensively reported upon in *The Field* during the same period when Linskill was writing about CUGC in the same newspaper. Gosset was also a good friend of Horace Hutchinson, the first Oxford captain, so it is strange that Linskill did not hear of Gosset's role in forming CUGC in 1869.

Andrew Graham Murray had become a member of the R&A in 1870 while he was still at Cambridge. His reputation both in legal and political circles meant that he became an important figure, and in 1892 he became the Captain of the R&A. Linskill would have known him and due to Linskill's extrovert character it is extremely unlikely that Graham Murray did not know of Linskill. They both appear in the famous large group painting which hangs in the R&A Big Room, *Medal Day at St Andrews 1894*.

The third man, Claude Carnegie was also a member of the R&A. Reports in *The Field* exist of Carnegie playing matches at St Andrews in 1874, 1875 and 1876 when Linskill was also playing there.

If ever there was an admission on Linskill's part that he knew of the earlier formation of the club, it appeared in a letter he had published in *Golf* on 9 January 1892:

> *A Westward Ho! golfer tells me that many years ago, when at Trinity College, he and a few friends used to go and play over the Heath, and that one of their best caddies was a strapping Royston lassie.*

This could not have been George Gosset as he had, by then, emigrated to New Zealand and, in any case, he went to King's College. But, Claude Carnegie, who was a Trinity man, had moved from Scotland to Devon by that time. So, Linskill and Carnegie must have spoken.

Perhaps a certain self-centredness in Linskill's character did not allow him to give up his 'I did it' position. This should not detract from what he did achieve in re-establishing the club in 1876. However, there is now strong enough evidence to date the formation of the Cambridge University Golf Club to 1869 rather than 1876, and certainly not to the usually-stated 1875, and thus placing it amongst the six oldest still-active clubs in England.

Linskill's role in getting the first Varsity match up and running in 1878 is much more unequivocal. None other than the captain of the Oxford side, Horace Hutchinson, said as much:

> *The institution of the Inter-University Golf Match was due to the genius (which we will define in this instance as the zeal and enterprise) of one of the very finest putters that ever put a ball into a hole, Mr. W.T. Linskill. Linskill was the inspiration of the golf at Cambridge, and he did a great deal more than any of us at Oxford to get the Oxford and Cambridge Golf Match going. We only followed.*[51]

It is worth reminding ourselves that the first Varsity match preceded the first Amateur Championship in 1885 by seven years. There is no older or longer-lived fixture in the English amateur golfing calendar. In March 2016, the 127th Varsity match was played at the Royal West Norfolk Golf Club at Brancaster.

Lastly, let us consider the importance of the Linskill presence over a twenty-year period at the heart of CUGC. The bare bones were as follows. He was the key figure from the outset in 1876. He was then captain over a seven-year period from 1876 to 1883. When he stepped down, it seems that he remained on the committee as its meetings were often reported to have taken place in his rooms. Then, in 1887 he became the honorary secretary, a position he held for a period of ten years, until he departed Cambridge to move to St Andrews in 1896.

He oversaw the evolution of the club from its humble beginnings when 11 golfers took part in the first competition at Coldham Common on 22 March 1876. No detailed statistics exist of the membership over time but an indication can be obtained from the various reports that appeared over the years. Between 1880 and 1885, the number of competitors in the Michaelmas terminal competition grew steadily from around 20 to 30. Following the opening of the 18-hole course in 1887, competition numbers increased to over 40. The highest recorded entry was 55 in November 1895.

In the first publication of *The Golfing Annual* for the year 1887-88, it was reported that CUGC had 120 members. This figure increased to 200 in 1889-90, to 300 in 1890-91, to 400 in 1891-92 and in the years 1892-93 and 1893-94, CUGC is reported to have 500 members. By this time, in England and Wales, only Royal Liverpool was larger with 684 members while St George's and Tooting Bec both reported that they also had about 500 members.

[51]Hutchinson H, *Fifty Years of Golf*, London, 1919

There was then a tailing off, with membership numbers nevertheless reported to be in excess of 400 in 1894-95 and 1895-96.

These astonishing figures in the boom period for CUGC are supported by the lists of new members elected which appear in the minute book for that era. In the year 1890-91, 93 new members joined in October and November 1890 alone; 83 new members in the same months in 1891; 81 new members in 1892; while 65 new members are recorded in the Michaelmas term of 1893.

While the growth rates seem credible, the overall membership numbers still seem surprisingly high in relation to the number of golfers playing in competitions. It could be that 'life members' are included in the overall numbers, or that for some membership of the club was predominantly social. However, it has not been possible to verify either of these possibilities.

The success of CUGC in terms of membership growth was not all down to Linskill. Interest in golf was growing at an incredibly rapid rate around the country (and around the world) at that time. In 1887-88, *The Golfing Annual* contained information on 195 clubs, while in 1894-95 the publication reported on 1000 clubs. One other key figure in the boom times was the captain in 1891-92 and 1892-93, John Low. Bernard Darwin noted that:

> *Nothing but the enthusiasm of Mr W T Linskill, then the perpetual Honorary Secretary of the Club, could have made a golf course there [at Coldham Common], and nothing but the social gifts of Mr John Low could have made people play there in positive crowds, as they did during his reign.*[52]

Linskill made other important contributions through his administrative skills. He provided a steady supply of professionals from 'North Britain' (as he liked to call Scotland) to meet the needs of the club in terms of course preparation, club provision and teaching the beginners. St Andrews men, Bob Martin (the ex-Open Champion), James Gourlay and Willie Duncan as well as Frank Park from Musselburgh all spent a number of winters working at Coldham Common.

Linskill oversaw the course extension from a 9-hole layout to an 18-hole one and worked hard behind the scenes to obtain permission to lay drainage to deal with the waterlogged land to make it playable. Without that, the 18-hole course would not have been a viable proposition and the huge growth in membership in the early 1890s would probably not have taken place.

Lastly, it must not be forgotten that Linskill played a key role in a matter that benefits CUGC and its members to this day. He initiated the relationship with

[52]Darwin B, *Green Memories, Cambridge Golf*, London, 1928

Worlington. Linskill, as was his way, got involved in a number of clubs in the vicinity of Cambridge. John Low and Linskill are purported to have laid out the course at Royston in 1892, where they both became founder members. In 1893, Linskill was on the committee at Chesterford Park Golf Club near Saffron Walden. And he was reported to be an honorary member and on the original Council at Worlington, also in 1893. In November 1893 he brought the CUGC captain, A M Chance, and several members of the CUGC committee over to Worlington for a game and to show them how good a course it was. A year later an arrangement was announced that allowed undergraduate members of CUGC to become temporary members of Worlington on payment of 10s/6d per term. Without Linskill's initiative this may not have happened and the close association between the two clubs might not have developed. It could be argued that this is the most important and long-lasting contribution that Linskill made and from which CUGC has benefitted ever since.

To complete this assessment of Linskill's qualities and his contribution to CUGC, it seems right to turn to two men who knew him well and were prepared to give an honest opinion.

First, from Bernard Darwin:

> *He was an honest, genuine, enthusiastic and kind-hearted man, but I am not prepared to say that his influence on the golfing undergraduate was an entirely good one … I must admit that I was rather relieved when he left Cambridge just before I became captain of the side for … he held rather arbitrary views.*

Darwin was polite and discreet enough not to go into details but clearly he felt that it was a good time for Linskill to move on to pastures new before he outstayed his welcome or tarnished his legacy in any way.

And to finish, John Low had this to say about the contribution made to Cambridge golf by his good friend W T Linskill:

> *For twenty years the Cambridge Club had the advantage of the services of its founder, Mr W T Linskill. In the later seventies Mr Linskill started as best he could, as captain, secretary, groundsman and sole member to play the Scottish game among a people who knew it hardly even by name … . When, in after years, the popularity of the pastime was assured, Mr Linskill still continued to give his entire services to the club; acting for twenty years in the capacity of Hon Secretary. As a financier he may have made mistakes, but they were far more over-balanced by the enthusiasm with which he instilled the members,*

and the energy he displayed in the work of the club. A man of leisure, he was able to devote his whole time to stirring up the undergraduates, and to giving them zeal for the cause he himself had at heart. Hardly a day passed but saw him bustling about, enquiring how the men were playing, or engaged in a friendly foursome with his more familiar friends. It can be easily understood that when Mr Linskill left Cambridge the Club lost a great stock of energy, the most important of commodities in a University society.

William T Linskill dressed for golf.

8

Coldham Common
– the decline and fall

From 1896-97 to 1901-02

1896-97

With Linskill having left Cambridge, it was all change amongst the senior officers of the club. Charles Pigg stepped down from being President after five years in the role and took over Linskill's position as honorary secretary. William Welsh became the new President of the club (and would remain so for the next three decades). As already noted, the new captain was Bernard Darwin.

Perhaps the first signs of decline in the membership had arrived, with only fourteen new members noted in the minute book as having joined the club in October 1896.

On 26 October 1896, the professional, Willie Duncan shot 72, a score 'likely to remain unbeaten for some time'. On the other hand, Duncan was in trouble for 'general dishonesty towards the club'. He was called before the committee to explain 'certain irregularities'. The minutes do not expand on this (as minutes rarely do), but he was retained and would remain *in situ* for another five years.

But this was Darwin's year. As well as being the captain, he won the Linskill Cup twice more and his handicap was reduced to +3, the first time that a CUGC golfer was deemed to be better than scratch. In the Varsity match he won for the third time in three years and by 7 holes in the top match. Cambridge needed that result to win overall by 16 holes to 11. The match was back at Sandwich again and it was noted in *The Cambridge Review* that:

> It is to be hoped that Sandwich will now become the permanent home of the match, being in every way infinitely preferable to Wimbledon or any other inland course as a real test of golf.

The view of the new hon sec, Charles Pigg, clearly differed from that of his predecessor.

1897-98

As the new academic year began, there was a sense of optimism in the hon sec's note to *The Cambridge Review*:

> *The University Golf course on Coldham Common is ready for play and, owing to the favourable [summer] season, is in far better order than is usually the case at this period of the year. The greens have been cut and well-rolled and every effort has been made to render the course as good as the nature of the soil and surroundings will allow.*

And yet, there also seemed to be a little nervousness when he added that:

> *Freshmen are informed that this is the only University Golf course and that a capacious Club House has been erected at considerable outlay.*

At that time, there was only one other golf course in Cambridge.[53] This was a 9-hole course on Granchester Meadows constructed by H J Gray and Sons, of Cambridge sports shop fame, in 1895. While it may have offered some convenience and more pleasant surroundings than Coldham Common, it was not popular with the general public due to the risk of being hit by a ball while out walking the path between Granchester and Cambridge. In any case, that course did not last long.

There was also mention of a nine-hole layout being considered at the University rifle butts which would run in the direction of Coton village to the west of Cambridge. We shall return to the significance of this development in due course.

In January 1898 it was reported that 'golf is decidedly on the increase at Coldham Common. The influx of members, both this term as well as last term, has been very large'. And yet, when the Linskill Cup, St Andrews Medal and Pirie Memento were played for in two divisions in mid-February, only 21 players participated compared to the 40-50 that had been relatively commonplace in recent years.

The Varsity match stayed at Sandwich in 1898, but the format changed; instead of 18-hole matches, 36-hole matches were adopted. As Darwin had remarked following his own first Varsity match at Sandwich in 1895, 'It seemed a long way to go to play but one round'. The result was much the same, Cambridge winning 11 holes up.

---

[53]There were, of course, others nearby, including Royston, Chesterford Park, St Neots and Royal Worlington and Newmarket. But a train journey was required to get to them.

1898-99

The new academic year got underway with a rash of low scoring:

> *A C Lawrence [the new captain] having lowered the record from 75 to 74 and P W Leathart [the immediate past captain] having been round three times in 75.*

This clearly referred to the amateur course record as the professional Willie Duncan had shot 73 in November 1895 and 72 in October 1896. In the Barrow Medal on 11 November, Leathart won 6 up on the Bogeyman. Not only that but he shot 73 to further lower the amateur course record. There was more low scoring in one of the weekly handicaps that term – F H Churchill won the Second Class sweep 'sending in a score that has never been equalled in the annals of the club' with an 85 less 16, giving a net 69. The hon sec clearly did not view this score as an aberration because a week later, Churchill was playing in the First Class sweep, now off a handicap of 6.

It was noted in the minutes that there was more than the average number of new members that term. It is unclear what 'average' meant. In the early 1890s, they were joining in the hundreds each year. Only 26 were recorded to have played on the Linskill Cup day on 4 November 1898.

On 14 November, CUGC played in its annual away match at Royal Blackheath. The overall result of the 8-aside match was a home victory with Blackheath 24 holes up to CUGC's 20 holes up. This fixture would not really merit much comment except for the result of one match – N F Hunter of CUGC beat Blackheath's W O S Pell, winning all 18 holes!

On 3 December 1898, CUGC played its first match against the recently formed Oxford and Cambridge Golfing Society (the Society). The Society had been created following a match against Oxford in December 1897. The first captain was John Low, the former Cambridge captain. Bernard Darwin, was also a founder member. The result of the match was 29 holes to the Society and 1 to CUGC, the solitary victory that of A C Lawrence over Low. The Society would subsequently play against both Oxford and Cambridge annually (as well as against other golf clubs and societies). These matches would come to act as a barometer to judge the relative capabilities of the two University sides prior to the Varsity match each year. CUGC also played matches against Old Cantabs and H M Braybrooke's team of former CUGC members. Low and Darwin often played in both of these matches also.

The portents of the match against the Society proved accurate, with Cambridge losing the last Varsity match of the nineteenth century by 18 holes. The two star players of the Cambridge team, P W Leathart and A C Lawrence, both lost. In an interesting symmetry, in the bottom two matches, representing Oxford, A H Leathart and C T Lawrence (both of New College) both won, and rather uncannily by a total of 18 holes. Bragging rights in the Leathart and Lawrence families would have belonged to the Oxford pair for they were the younger brothers of the Cambridge pair!

In December 1898, the professional Willie Duncan had been approached by the Bursar of Gonville and Caius College to mark out a new 18-hole golf course on land owned by the College on the Gog Magog hills to the south-east of the town. This he did for the princely sum of £1 (about a week's wages). In 1899 the first nine greens were prepared.

If there was any need to emphasise further the class of those who attended the University as undergraduates, it could be found in March 1899 when the militia were camping on Coldham Common. Whilst there, the officers (but not the men) were offered the use of the CUGC clubhouse.

1899-1900

At the commencement of the Michaelmas term, Willie Duncan was still the professional at Coldham Common, supported by a greenkeeper, J Spaxman, who was putting the links 'in excellent order'. So excellent in fact that a new course record was set on 25 October 1899. The new Captain, E E Apthorp, lowered Leathart's record of 73 by 4 shots, as follows:

4 4 2 4 4 4 5 4 4 = 35 out
4 3 4 3 4 3 4 4 5 = 34 home
           69 total

It would never be beaten.

In November 1899, a new policeman was engaged to keep 'the caddies and loafers' around the ditch at the 16th hole (and elsewhere) under control to prevent them from interfering 'in anyway with the members when they were playing on the Links'. The ruffians from Barnwell clearly remained a persistent problem.

The result of the match against the Society in December 1899 was similar to that in the previous year; CUGC lost by 37 holes. It did not augur well for the Varsity match which was due to be played in March 1900 at Sandwich against a very strong Oxford side. In fact the defeat, when it came, could not have been more resounding. Cambridge did not win a match all day and lost 69 holes down.

1900-01

As term began, the hon sec was once more drawn to remind freshmen that Coldham Common was 'the only University Golf course and that a capacious Club House and Bicycle Shed have been erected at considerable outlay'. While the Granchester Meadows course might have been seen off, the Gonville and Caius inspired course on the Gog Magog hills was now beginning to take shape. By January 1901 nine more greens had been laid and the full 18-hole course was brought into use in March 1901. Meanwhile the 1895 arrangement made with Worlington (i.e. temporary membership for 10s/6d per term) was still in place.

In October 1900, A F Dudgeon (Trinity) was elected captain for the year. However in December he announced that he would have to resign his post. W G Howarth was unanimously elected in his stead. The outgoing captain received a vote of thanks and congratulations on his appointment. *Alumni Cantabrigienses* reported that he was employed at the Guinness brewery in Dublin in 1901.

Golf at Coldham Common was always challenging. No less so when the rifle range was in use. Charles B L Tennyson, a grandson of Alfred Lord Tennyson, was a member of CUGC between 1899 and 1902. He related the following story about how the rifle range would sometimes interfere with golf:

> *The only hazard beside the ditches, which were made to guard about one-third of the holes, was the town rifle range. This ran down the middle of the course, and, when in use, constituted a very real danger, for at two or three holes an errant ball had often to be retrieved under rifle-fire occasionally supplemented by a machine-gun, the shells of which hurtled over one's head with a kind of flapping hiss peculiarly disquieting to a man of peaceful temperament.*

Darwin had much the same to say:

> *If you sliced onto the butts when shooting was going on, you waved your red coat as a danger signal and walked into the danger zone to play your shot. That is if you were brave. If you weren't you abandoned it to its fate.*

For the Barrow Medal played on 7 March 1901, it was reported that:

> *As the [rifle] range on the Common was being used a special nine hole course had to be arranged, for which a bogey of 39 was fixed.*

This was probably a wise move. Golf went on and J B Escolme won the Barrow Medal, in a field of 20, beating Colonel Bogey 1 up.

In preparation for the 1901 Varsity match, CUGC played seven matches during the Lent term against Great Yarmouth, Royal Blackheath, West Herts., Mid-Surrey, Eltham, Old Cantabs and Woking. They lost the lot. Interestingly, the match against Blackheath was a home one, but instead of being played at Coldham Common, arrangements were made to play at Worlington. A portent of things to come.

Oxford, on the other hand, had only lost one match all year to 'a very strong team of Scotch golfers captained by Mr T Mansfield Hunter'. On this basis, an easy victory was predicted for Oxford. It spoke volumes that their winning score of 19 holes up was considered to be a good performance by Cambridge. It was now Oxford who were in the ascendancy having won three matches in a row and all by convincing margins.

The heydays of the early-to-mid-1890s now seemed like an age ago. Membership had declined and so too had the quality of the golfers. As a result the upper hand that Cambridge once held over Oxford had been reversed. Coldham Common was becoming a less and less attractive place to play and now there was a new course in Cambridge, about to open in a rather more scenic setting on the nearby chalk hills of Gog Magog. It was time to act and make important decisions. And those decisions would have a profound impact on the path chosen by the Cambridge University Golf Club as the new century got underway.

1901-02

At CUGC's first meeting of the new academic year in late October 1901, Ernest Hill-Thomson (Pembroke) was elected as the new captain. Charles Pigg was still the hon sec, while Hubert F H Caldwell (Trinity) was the assistant hon sec. At the meeting, Pigg made a short statement with regard to the balance sheet, which showed that the club was in a very sound financial position, the debt of the clubhouse having been finally paid off. However, at almost exactly the same time, the Gonville and Caius inspired Gog Magog golf club was being formed with an initial 150 subscribers. The founder members consisted of '110 gentlemen, 19 ladies and about 20 undergraduates'.[54] It was this third category that was highly controversial on two counts: first, because it drew undergraduates away from joining CUGC and second, because, one of the terms of the lease agreement stated that:

> *The Club undertakes … that the links should be used primarily as a place of recreation for the resident graduate members of the University and that they will not allow this purpose to be defeated by reason of the number of undergraduates or non-members of the University admitted to the Club.*

[54]*The Minutes of the Gog Magog Golf Club*, 22 October 1901.

101

Furthermore, undergraduates, as associate members, would have no voting rights in the management of the club and their number would 'be fixed from time to time by the Committee'.

Why would the College stipulate this in the lease? The most likely explanation is that CUGC had always been dominated by the interests of the undergraduates and that the few dons who were members had very little say in matters there. So, the Gogs would become the preserve of the dons, whilst the admission of undergraduates seemed to be more to do with balancing the books.

On 31 October, *The Cambridge Review* included the following editorial comment:

> *The new golf course on the Gogmagog Hills seems to be gaining on Coldham in popularity. Reports as to the condition of the green are conflicting, but there is every reason for thinking that the turf will be made more suitable for the game than that of the present course, and the progress made up to the present is decidedly encouraging. Whether the University Club will migrate or not remains to be seen.*

Things then began to move at a fairly rapid pace. On 14 November it was reported in *The Cambridge Review* that:

> *The CUGC have just made an agreement with the Royal Washington [sic] and Newmarket Golf Club by which all members of the University Club will be allowed to play free of charge on the excellent 9 hole course at Mildenhall .... Inter-club matches will in future be played at Mildenhall, a change which will doubtless be welcomed by our visitors, who do not see Coldham at its best in December or the early spring.*

The agreement, it transpires, was that for a block annual payment of £15, CUGC undergraduates could play at Worlington. This took the 1895 arrangement between CUGC and Worlington to another level. Furthermore, by moving all future fixtures to Worlington, it was an additional nail in the coffin for Coldham Common.

The Worlington deal may have been an attractive one for CUGC but it still took a train journey for its members to get there rather than a cycle ride to the Gogs. On 21 November, a letter from Reverend John Lock, the Bursar at Gonville and Caius appeared in *The Cambridge Review* informing the readership that:

> *These links may now be said to have emerged from the experimental stage, having been definitely taken over by a club called the Gogmagog Golf Club.*

A week later (28 November), the editor published a lengthy riposte from the CUGC captain, Hill-Thomson. The gist of his response was as follows:

> *To judge from the glowing description of the Gogmagog Golf Links in your last issue, it might be inferred that no such thing as the Cambridge University Golf Club was in existence.*
>
> *We wish to agree with the promoters in their laudable desire to encourage the game of golf among the graduate members of the University, but we emphatically wish to protest against their admitting undergraduate members to their club to the serious detriment of the University Golf Club.*
>
> *After being hampered by debt [due to the construction of the clubhouse] for so many years, the University Club is now able to offer to its members the high privilege of playing without any fee, over one of the finest inland courses in the Kingdom (Mildenhall); but at the same time this University Club of twenty-five years standing, receives a severe blow from what is plainly a mere private speculation on the part of a College.*
>
> *We have written this letter in order that undergraduates may realise their true position with regard to the Gogmagog Club.*

A robust response indeed.

Meanwhile back on the golf course, on 30 November 1901, CUGC played its first home match at Worlington, although since it was against the Society, it was more or less a home match for both sides. It brought no change in fortunes for CUGC who won 1 hole, but lost 55. Perhaps off-course matters were acting as a distraction?

In these challenging days for CUGC, the approaching Christmas vacation offered a welcome break. It would be a time of festive cheer but possibly also provide the opportunity for some much-needed calm moments for reflection.

As the Lent term in 1902 got underway, maybe some informal conversations had begun to take place between golfing dons and undergraduates. Whatever transpired, there were some early signs of rapprochement between CUGC and the Gogs. In the Gogs' committee minutes for 25 January 1902, Dr Alan Gray reported that CUGC had approached him and suggested that the members of the University team be granted permission to play at the Gogs during the Lent term and would also be willing to pay for the privilege.[55] The committee decided to

---

[55] Alan Gray was the organist at Trinity College from 1893 to 1930. He was also a member of the R&A. He was very recognisable whether in Cambridge or St Andrews – a giant of a man, 6ft 6 ½ inches tall. He would become the second Captain of the Gog Magog Golf Club in 1902.

allow the team (not exceeding 12 members) to practice at the Gogs, but without payment. When news of this arrangement reached *The Cambridge Review* on 6 February, the editor commented that:

> *This is very pleasing news and it certainly shows that the Gog Magog Club is not inimical to the interests of University Golf. We trust that this graceful action on the part of the new Club will lead to further developments. It seems clear that amalgamation in some form or other would be to the advantage of everybody.*

In reference to this latter point, the Gogs minutes from 25 January also recorded that Dr Gray reported:

> *….an interview [he] had had with Mr Caldwell, the Sec of the CUGC at which it was proposed by the University Club that they should amalgamate with this Club and the proposed basis of such amalgamation was discussed and a letter was read from Mr Caldwell suggesting that this Club should draw up proposals for the consideration of the University Club.*

After a few more meetings and 'with certain amendments suggested by the captain and secretary of the CUGC', the final heads of agreement were prepared. The Gogs minutes of 25 February 1902 contain a memorandum to be adopted 'as a basis of further communication with the Officials of the CUGC':

> *Subject to the settlement of the amount to be allowed to the University Club for Team expenses &c and subject to the control of the ground men being in the hands of the Secretaries of the GMGC, the Committee of the GMGC are favourable to the proposals of the University Club. They would venture to point out that before Coldham can be deserted the Trustees of the Pavilion ought to be consulted. Any proposal will of course have to be accepted by a general meeting of the GMGC and the great inducement that the Committee will place before the General Meeting will be the agreement that undergraduates will only have the right to play on the second course.*

So there we have it. Coldham Common would be abandoned and CUGC would move to the Gogs but only to play, in effect, on their own course, the second course, which was being laid out at that time. It was an amalgamation, but not on equal terms. CUGC would in essence be a club within a club and presumably also on an inferior course.

The next important development took place on Thursday 6 March. It was announced that same day in *The Cambridge Review* that:

A general meeting will be held … in the Lion Hotel, the President, Mr W Welsh (Jesus) in the Chair. As matters of great importance to the University Club will be discussed, it is hoped that as many members as possible will make a point of being present. The matters under discussion will also appeal to all Cambridge Golfers, and the Committee of the CUGC will be glad to see at the meeting any members of the University, irrespective of their belonging to the CUGC.

On 13 March, the full details of the general meeting were published in *The Cambridge Review*:

The past few weeks have been eventful ones for Cambridge golfers. The University Club recognised that they were too heavily handicapped with the squalid state of Coldham, and realised that negotiations with the Gog Magog Club were impolitic. They have acted with great energy and secured an admirable piece of ground in a beautiful situation on Whitwell Hill close to Coton, 2 ½ miles from Cambridge. The ground was inspected yesterday (i.e. 12 March) by Mr A R Paterson, late President, OUBC and at present Convener of the Green Committee on the championship course of the Hon Company at Muirfield, with Willie Park junr., the well-known ex-champion golfer. They report most favourably of the possibilities of making, at comparatively small expense, a really sporting course.

The CUGC committee presented two options to its members: either to amalgamate with the Gog Magog golf club but only with access to the second 18-hole course, or to build the new course at Whitwell Hill, Coton and to obtain a lease from King's College. The arguments in favour of the latter option must have been compelling because it was carried unanimously.

All of this must have come as a huge surprise to the Gogs committee. There are no references in the club's minutes that indicate that they knew anything about the proposed course at Coton prior to the 6 March meeting. But the CUGC committee must have invested considerable time and effort to create this alternative. It is unknown how and when the Coton land had been identified; King's College must have participated in confidential discussions with CUGC without any leaks emerging to King's fellows who were Gogs members. A letter dated Friday 28 February 1902 was discovered in King's College archives from the assistant honorary secretary of CUGC, HFH Caldwell, to the second bursar at King's, William Macaulay, with reference to the Coton land. It said:

> *We are all going over to see the spot [Whitwell Hill] on Sunday [2 March] and I shall write further.*

Furthermore, the Edinburgh-based Paterson, and Huntercombe-based Willie Park Jr., had been contacted and arranged to come to Cambridge to inspect it. Clearly all of this must have encompassed several weeks, during which time CUGC had been in earnest negotiations with the Gogs regarding amalgamation.

The article in *The Cambridge Review* on 13 March provided some further information about the swift pace of development planned for the new course at Coton:

> *Willie Duncan, the University Club professional, with one of Gowan's assistants from Mildenhall, will start work on the new course next Monday. They will devote their attention entirely to laying out nine holes in the first instance, as selected by Willie Park. Mr J MacDonald, FRHS [Fellow of the Royal Horticultural Society], turf specialist, is to visit the new links today in order to advise as to the treatment of the putting greens. The University Golf Club will have the use of Mildenhall, as usual, next term, and it is confidently anticipated that the new ground will be in first-class order by October.*

Willie Park Jr was a major figure in the golfing world at that time. He was born in Musselburgh and his family was steeped in golf. His father, Willie Park Senior, won the Open Championship four times between 1860 and 1875, his uncle Mungo Park won it in 1874 and Willie Jr himself won it twice, in 1887 and 1889. But he is probably now even better known as a golf course architect having designed or improved around 170 courses in the UK, Europe and North America. In 1901 alone, the year before his visit to Coton, three courses that he designed were opened – Sunningdale (Old), Huntercombe and Hollinwell (Notts Golf Club).

James MacDonald was of Scottish origin and had started his own business with his sons as nurserymen in Harpenden, but then made a speciality of improving the quality of turf used on golf courses. Today he would be called a golf course agronomist.

In the midst of all this drama, the Linskill Cup, St Andrews Medal and Pirie Memento competitions had been played on the same day as the general meeting. It would be the last time that the terminal competition would be held at Coldham, a quarter of a century since it had all begun there. As a reflection of the times, only a handful of members participated as the competition clashed with the third day of the Lent Bumps.[56] For the record, G Hoffmann won the last Linskill Cup competition played at Coldham Common with a score of 90; there was a tie between G Hoffmann, A L Hetherington and T H Davies for the St Andrews Medal; and J Barber won the Pirie Memento.

On 24 April, *The Cambridge Review* provided an update on progress at Whitwell Hill:

We are pleased to report that the work at the new links of the University Golf Club is now well under way ..... The University professional [W Duncan], and an assistant from Mildenhall, have been at work for over a month, and already the greens are looking most promising. It is hoped that by next October, when the new course will be opened, there will be a large increase in the membership of the University Club.

The article also noted that the Oxford University club had a membership of over 400 undergraduates, with a waiting list of 30. No wonder Oxford had won the previous three Varsity encounters so comfortably. It was the same story on 25 March 1902 with Oxford victorious by 52 holes to 5 and winning seven of the eight matches played. For Cambridge, clearly a new way forward was needed.

The end of Coldham Common, when it came, was fairly swift. At a meeting of the club on 6 May, the members were asked to vote on three resolutions: (1) that the links at Coldham be abandoned and play be transferred to Whitwell Hill, and that the Committee be empowered to arrange a lease of that ground; (2) that authority be given to the Committee to dispose of the Coldham pavilion and house by sale or lease; and (3) that the Committee be empowered to raise a special subscription to meet the expenses of laying out the new ground.

The resolutions were unanimously approved. In a letter to the members, the reasons for abandoning Coldham Common were given succinctly:

... play has greatly diminished at Coldham, and the number of new members has fallen off in spite of the increased number of players in the University. The unattractive nature of the course and its depressing surroundings made it hopeless to continue, and a change to a new course, in a pleasanter locality and more completely under the control of the Club as to the making of greens and the construction of hazards, will conduce, it is hoped, to the prosperity of the Club and provide better opportunities of play for its members.

[56]Inter-college boat races on the River Cam.

The letter continued with an appeal to members, past and present, to provide the necessary £500 to invest in the development of the new course at Whitwell Hill. A life membership of the club was on offer for a subscription of five guineas.

On 25 May, the CUGC minutes note that 'it was resolved that Duncan be dismissed'. He had been the head professional for seven years, but it seemed that there was no desire to keep him on as the professional at the new course at Whitwell Hill.

A sub-committee was formed to handle all the arrangements for the new course. The lease of the land from King's College was signed on 17 June 1902. William Welsh and Charles Pigg together with two other dons were the trustees on behalf of the Cambridge University Golf Club. The land consisted of 35 acres adjacent to the road between Coton and Granchester. The plan of the land that appears in the lease is consistent with the enclosed fields which are part of Rectory Farm today. The lease was for fourteen years – the first seven (1902-1909) at a rent of £25 per annum and the second seven (1909-1916) at a rent of £30 per annum. It was also reported that overtures were being made to Clare College to lease adjacent land in order to extend the course to a full 18 holes.

A separate committee was formed to arrange for the disposal of the Coldham Pavilion. This took a little longer to resolve. But at the general meeting of the club on 20 October 1902, it was announced that the clubhouse had been sold for £300 less expenses. This was clearly at a substantial loss when compared with the £1,000 raised to construct it and fit it out in 1890.

And with that, it was the end of golf at Coldham Common, the worst course that Bernard Darwin had ever seen. But in nostalgic reflection, he had the following to say about it:

> *I have not painted an engaging picture, and yet, if anyone else should attack it too venomously, I still feel a sort of loyalty to Coldham. "How for everything there is a time and a season, and then how does a glory of a thing pass from it, even like the flower of the grass." Coldham is gone and could never return, but it was good fun in its time.*

9

Coton – a fresh start

From 1902-03 to 1918-19

1902-03

On 16 October 1902, the following editorial item appeared in *The Cambridge Review*:

> *We are pleased to learn that the undergraduates have responded splendidly to the efforts of the University Golf Club Committee to provide them with a desirable course; over forty new members have already joined this term. Report, moreover, reaches us that the new course on Whitwell Hill is in excellent condition. It is difficult to believe that it has only been in hand for some six months. Mr MacDonald, the turf specialist, has done wonders with the putting greens and after Christmas he hopes to have them quite perfect.*

The CUGC minutes note that Robert Glass of North Berwick had been appointed as the professional. He was noted to be a competent teacher with an excellent assortment of clubs and balls. Research has uncovered no further information about him.

In the next edition of *The Cambridge Review* (23 October), it was reported that over 80 new members had now joined. With this substantial intake providing necessary finance, the club entered into negotiations with Clare College to lease additional land to extend the course to a full 18 holes. The lease with Clare College has not been uncovered. However, it is reported in *British History Online* that:

> *By 1905 c.77a. probably on the north slope of Barton down, was temporarily occupied by the University Golf Club.*

Given that the lease of the King's land was for 35 acres, this suggests that the Clare land amounted to around 40 acres. Overall, this would be quite adequate to lay out an eighteen-hole course.

The first competition took place on Whitwell Hill, a weekly sweepstake, on 17 October 1902. R C Simpson won with 97 less 10 for a net 87 over twenty holes (twice around the ten-hole course). After the Christmas break, it was announced (22 January 1903) that:

> *The full course (18 holes) at Whitwell Hill is now ready for play. The new ground is admirably adapted for the game, and the arrangement of holes fits in nicely with the course opened last term. Under W MacDonald's care the greens have come on wonderfully, and before very long the whole course will compare favourably with the best of inland courses.*

Interestingly, Bernard Darwin in his seminal work, *The Golf Courses of the British Isles* published in 1910, said:

> *Coton I do not know well, but though an enthusiastic captain of Cambridge once told me that the greens were as good as the best seaside ones, I am disposed to think he was romancing.*

During this time, college golf clubs started to form. Trinity took the lead with over 40 members, with King's, Clare and Pembroke following suit. On 14 October at Whitwell Hill, Trinity beat Pembroke by 16 holes. It was announced that this was the first ever inter-college match in Cambridge. In fact, this was not quite the case. On 28 October 1868, 'a friendly match' was reported to have taken place on Therfield Heath at Royston between Trinity and King's in which Andrew Graham Murray of Trinity 'stood alone' (in the absence of Claude Carnegie) against George Gosset and Cecil Kellner of King's. Also, there was an occasion at Coldham Common in 1879 when Trinity College took on a 'rest of the University' side.

On 26 February 1903, it was reported that 'the annual competitions for the Linskill Cup (scratch), the Pirie Memento and the St Andrews Cross (both under handicap), took place at Whitwell Hill on Thursday, February 19th'. This was the first time that the competitions had been 'annual'. From their commencement in 1876, they had been 'terminal', i.e. three times per year. In more recent times this was reduced to twice a year at Coldham Common due to the long grass in the Easter term.

While the new course at Whitwell Hill was proving an attraction, the arrangement with Royal Worlington and Newmarket was an additional incentive to join the club. As may be recalled, the original arrangement was, for an annual fee of £15, there was no upper limit on the number of undergraduates who could go there to play golf. Conscious that this was a very good deal, and while still desirous to retain the arrangement, the club accepted an increase in the block fee to £20.

Meanwhile, as per its agreement, the University side continued to play all its home fixtures at Worlington. That Lent term in 1903, there were matches against Old Cantabs, Worlington itself and the Society. A new away fixture was established in March 1903, against Sunningdale which included in their side, H S Colt, the new club's first secretary. Cambridge was victorious by 14 holes to 12. It did not seem to help matters in the annual Varsity match however, as Oxford won again to extend their winning run to five.

1903-04

As the new term commenced in 1903, the club seemed to be in good health. New members continued to join, albeit not at the rate of the previous year, and the course at Whitwell Hill was in fair condition. However, as was the case at Coldham Common, there were times when waterlogging was a problem. Draining was undertaken to improve the course. Plans were made to erect a large room for members and a bicycle shed.

College-based golf was also thriving; Clare now had a membership of over 30 and had instituted a College Cup to be played for using 'the Calcutta Cup system'.

Because of the growth in membership, the Worlington agreement was coming under some strain as too many undergraduates were taking advantage of the privilege it conferred. As a result of this, yet another new arrangement was put in place in December 1903 in which members of CUGC could join Worlington as honorary members for a subscription of 10s/6d per year, with CUGC guaranteeing a sum equal to forty such subscriptions. In this way, Worlington was guaranteed £21 with an additional 10s/6d for each CUGC member above forty. This would also provide CUGC with the right to continue to play its matches at Worlington.

In the match at Sunningdale in February 1904, as well as H S Colt playing for the home side, a certain R Graham Murray did so. In all likelihood, this was Major Ronald Thomas Graham Murray who was the only son of Andrew Graham Murray (soon to become Lord Dunedin). Like his father, he must have been an able golfer as he won his match 8 holes up.

Despite the influx of members, CUGC's finances were still worrisome. The honorary treasurer reported in May 1904 that bills amounting to £150 had not been paid and that another £100 was due by 1 October. To deal with this, it was decided to use £150 of the money raised from the sale of the Coldham clubhouse (i.e. £300) to meet current expenses. It was also decided 'to make further appeals for subscriptions'. This included appeals to past members for donations.

Although the Varsity match in 1904 resulted in another win for Oxford to extend their run to six, it was a closer run affair, the margin being only 2 holes. Perhaps the tide was turning?

1904-05

In the first weekly competition of the new academic year, two players, G Hoffman (the captain) and M T Allen, shot 72 to reduce the course record at Whitwell Hill by four shots. Within a fortnight, G Hoffman lowered the record a further shot to 71. In Michaelmas term 1904, competitions took place for the Linskill Cup, the Pirie Memento, the St Andrews Medal and the Barrow Medal. Reverting back to earlier practice, the Linskill Cup and Pirie Memento were played for again in the Lent term.

In 1905, the Varsity match was played at Sunningdale for the first time. Perhaps some familiarity of the course helped Cambridge now that they played an annual match there against the home club. Also, six of the eight Cambridge men played in the previous year's match, whereas only two of the Oxford team reappeared. Whatever the explanation, Cambridge won resoundingly, 52 holes to 3, and only lost one of the seven matches. The tide had finally turned.

1905-06

On 26 October 1905 the usual beginning-of-year article appeared in *The Cambridge Review* reporting on the general meeting at which the officers for the year ahead were elected and dates for forthcoming fixtures announced. It was also reported with a slight sense of *déjà vu* that 'owing to the lack of accommodation at the club's present quarters, the Committee have been authorised to proceed with the erection of a new and spacious club room'. Prudently, the Committee decided to spend no more than £150 this time around and in the end agreed a contract to proceed with it for £140.

The next article to appear in *The Cambridge Review*, on 9 November, reported on CUGC's first match of the season away to Royston. The top home player was William Welsh, the eminent former Cambridge player and the then CUGC President. In most matches on his home territory at Royston he would be the favourite, but on this occasion he was up against it for his opponent in the top match was 'the amateur champion making his first appearance for Cambridge'.

The Amateur (as it was widely known) was first held in 1885. Horace Hutchinson, who played for Oxford in the first Varsity match in 1878, was the runner-up to Allan Macfie but then won the next two championships in 1886 and 1887. Other great Amateur Champions of that era included Johnny Ball and Harold Hilton of Hoylake and the Scots Johnny Laidlaw and Freddie Tait. The 1904 Amateur was won by an American for the first time, Walter J Travis, who had also won three US Amateur Championships. The 1905 Amateur Championship was held at Prestwick on hard fairways under a hot sun and by the end of the second day, Ball, Hilton, Hutchinson and Laidlaw had all been beaten.

By the end of the week, the winner, by 3&2 in the final, was a 19 year old St Andrews University student, Arthur Gordon Barry, the youngest champion to date. Darwin described his swing as 'fine, careless rapture'. Although studying at St Andrews, and also a member of the R&A, Gordon Barry was not a Scot. He was born in Cornwall of English parents who had moved to St Andrews when he was 13. He had had no formal golf lessons but had learned by watching and playing with some of the greats at St Andrews of that era, Andrew Kirkaldy and Laurie Auchterlonie. One of his good friends at St Andrews University, Peter C Anderson, had also won the Amateur title, in 1893. So, having won the championship himself, he went to Cambridge to continue his studies. Back at Royston on 2 November 1905, Welsh put up a valiant fight, only losing at the last hole to the Amateur Champion.

The Varsity match in 1906 was held at Hoylake for the first time and large crowds turned out to watch. It was estimated that the top match between A G Barry for Cambridge and G E Grundy of Oxford was followed by a crowd of around five hundred. Their match was halved. Incidentally, Gordon Barry's brother, Charles, also played in the match for Cambridge that year. He won his match by 2 holes. Overall Cambridge won by 30 holes to 7.

1906-07

In October 1906 the course at Coton was in good order. Several new tees had been constructed during the summer months and some new bunkers were also being contemplated. However, worms on the greens seemed to be a problem, as reported in *The Cambridge Review*:

> *Worm killer is being put down on several of the greens with excellent results. The number and size of these pests has hitherto militated against the growth of the finer species of grass.*

A subsequent article referred to the worms, 'or rather boa-constrictors, which littered the greens'. So the battle continued.

The usual competitions for the Linskill Cup, the St Andrews Medal, the Pirie Memento and the Barrow Medal took place in November and in February at Whitwell Hill.

CUGC members returned some excellent scores when they went over to play at Worlington. It was reported that M T Allen, the captain, had gone round in 74, lowering the previous record by two shots which stood jointly to the credit of G Hoffman (captain of CUGC in 1904-05) and J Humphries, the local professional. It was also recorded in the CUGC minutes about a week later that A G Barry 'had equalled his own record of the course, going round in 70'. It is not entirely clear how to reconcile these two statements.

The Varsity match in 1907 was again played at Hoylake, with Cambridge winning a close encounter 23 holes up against 22. The Barry brothers both played again, but on this occasion both lost, and by a total of 13 holes. To counter this M T Allen won 13 holes up. The overall result, apparently, depended on a single putt on the last green. With one match halved, Oxford had won 4 matches to Cambridge's 3. There had been other occasions in the past when one side had won the overall match (i.e. on a holes up basis) while winning fewer individual matches. However, following the 1907 result, it was decided that the 1908 match would be based on individual matches won rather than the aggregate number of holes up. And, that is how it remains to this day.

1907-08

In recent years a trial match had been played in October at Worlington between the captain's side and the hon sec's side. However, in 1907, 'owing to the great improvement in the course at Coton it was decided to hold a trial match there'. Disappointingly, owing to heavy rain the day before 'the grass on the greens was rather abundant, making very firm putting necessary, and there was a tendency not to be up'.

On 7 November it was reported in *The Cambridge Review* that 'it is a noticeable fact that the mathematics of the members of the club is very inferior'. Measures had to be taken to bring in more income and it was decided to allow non-members to play at Coton, except on Fridays, for 1s/6d for a round or 2s/6d for the day.

Sometime during Michaelmas term 1907, Harry S Colt must have visited the Whitwell Hill course because on 23 January 1908 it was reported that in accordance with his proposals, ten new bunkers had been added to the course. Interestingly, he must have been doing the same at Sunningdale at around the same time. It was also noted that:

> Although these new bunkers may not please the heart of all members none of them will regret to find that the hedge at the 2nd hole has been abolished and several new tees made.

On 6 March 1908, the St Andrews Medal was played for and won by G H Greathead with 85–9, net 76. This was the last occasion in which it was reported to have been played for. It may be recalled that since 1893, the St Andrews Medal had been a handicap competition for low handicappers while the Pirie Memento was for high handicappers. In the years following 1908, when results were reported, it seemed that the Pirie Memento was open to all members as a handicap competition. This would infer that it had been decided to 'retire' the St Andrews Medal, maybe due to the declining number of members of the club. Alternatively, it went missing. The medal, made by 'Morris of Kings Parade' had first been played for in March 1890. Its whereabouts remains unknown to this day.

The 1908 Varsity match was played at Sunningdale. Under the new system, Cambridge won by 4 matches to 3 with one match halved. That made it four wins on the trot for Cambridge to somewhat offset the six consecutive wins by Oxford prior to this.

1908-09

At the beginning of the new academic year, the fall in membership was reported to have left the club in debt by £178. Strictures were required and so it was decided not to carry out any extra work on the course during the year ahead.

On 6 November 1908, the Barrow Medal competition was held at Whitwell Hill. The winner was J F Ireland (Trinity) who, playing off scratch, was 5 up on Colonel Bogey and in the process set a course record of 72.[57] John Ireland was a Worlington member where a multitude of Irelands were members. His uncle Freddie had been a stalwart of Blackheath before moving his family to the Worlington area where he practised as a solicitor. J F Ireland was one of the outstanding amateur sportsmen of his generation. As well as representing Cambridge against Oxford at golf on three occasions, he did the same at hockey and on four occasions at cricket. Moreover, he was elected captain in all three sports.

Ireland lost his first Varsity match (but won in the following two) and Cambridge lost overall to Oxford by 6 matches to 2 at Royal St George's in 1909.

1909-10

The financial circumstances of CUGC had improved as a result of the austerity measures of the previous year combined with increased subscriptions at the start of Michaelmas 1909 – the deficit was reduced from £178 to £27. It was decided that the club had to spend money to improve the course at Whitwell Hill in order to attract more members. To this end, Colt's report (which he had prepared two years earlier) was reviewed. The CUGC minutes contain the following:

> *On Tuesday Oct 19 a green committee was held at Coton attended by Messrs Pigg [hon sec], Ulyat [captain] and Campbell [assistant hon sec]. The Course was inspected and several of the alterations suggested in Mr H S Colt's report on the course were agreed to.*

[57]From this it could also be concluded that Bogey for the course was probably about 77, which was not atypical for the times.

It was decided that no alteration should as yet be made to the 2nd or 4th but that after the 10th there should be a short hole (length 150 yds) running parallel to the 5th; that the next hole should return [parallel] to the present 10th up to the boundary hedge (length 300 yds); that the new 12th should be played from near the hedge to the present 12th green (length 430 yds). The present 11th green should no longer be used and also the present 15th should be left out and that the new 16th should be played from the present 15th tee to the present 16th green.

Although this tells us very little about the course at Whitwell Hill, it is the only fragment of a description that we have of it.

On 16 November 1909, the Barrow Medal was won by E J Hunter (Clare). Playing off a handicap of 1 he finished all square with Colonel Bogey. No further reports or references to the Barrow Medal appear in either *The Cambridge Review* or the CUGC Minute books. As referred to earlier, the Medal was purchased via auction at Bonham's in June 2011 by a golf collector, Mr Jim McCormick from Chicago.

By coincidence, a new medal was presented to CUGC in December 1909 by Royal Worlington, to be played for at Worlington off scratch. Initially it was called the Scratch Medal, then it became known as the Trotter Medal (after the Secretary at Worlington in that era) and then from 1936 it was re-named the Worlington Medal. The first winner was W E Gardner Beard with a 79.

1910-14

Over the period from 1910 to 1914, the reports about CUGC in *The Cambridge Review* focused almost entirely on matches against other clubs, most of which were played away. It was an extensive and attractive fixture list, including the likes of Norwich, Great Yarmouth, Ipswich, Brancaster, Stoke Poges, Mid Surrey, Richmond, Woking, Coombe Hill, Royal Wimbledon, Sunningdale, Walton Heath and Worplesdon. There was also the annual match held against the Society at Worlington. More often than not the other clubs would have past members of CUGC playing for them against their old university; Darwin in particular, who was a member of many clubs and golfing societies, would play two or three times a year against his *alma mater*.

While these fixtures were undoubtedly great fun, there was serious business at the end of the season to be dealt with. Ultimately these matches existed to help the captain identify his best players, and those who were on form, so that he could select his team to face up to Oxford in the Varsity match.[58]

---

[58] As remains the case to this day.

The 1910 Varsity match at Hoylake resulted in a 5-3 win for Cambridge. In 1911 at Rye the result was also 5-3 but this time in favour of Oxford. The fact that the two sides in this period were very closely matched was exemplified by the results in 1912 at Prince's and in 1913 at Hoylake, both ending in halved matches, 4-4. On completion of the 1913 match, the overall position in the full series of matches since 1878 was Oxford, 16 wins, Cambridge 16 wins, 3 drawn matches and 1 cancelled.[59] In order to increase the likelihood of obtaining a result one way or the other, it was agreed to change the format from 8-aside to 9-aside.

When the two teams arrived at Rye on 3 April 1914 there was a familiar face: A G Barry, the former Amateur Champion from 1905 who played for Cambridge in 1906 and 1907. However in 1914 he was now playing for Oxford having gone back to study at Oriel College. He was until 2016, the only man to have played for both sides in the Varsity match.[60] Barry's switching sides was criticised in certain quarters, Darwin amongst them, so there may have been some satisfaction in seeing him lose 6&5. With eight matches played the scores were level at 4-4. It would all boil down to the crucial new ninth match which was between H B Stokoe (Oriel) and O Lyttelton (Trinity). In an encounter which swung to and fro, Stokoe became the hero winning at the 17th hole in the afternoon to win the match overall for Oxford.

However, the outcome of the Varsity match soon paled into insignificance. On 28 June the Archduke Franz Ferdinand was assassinated in Sarajevo and on 4 August 1914 Britain declared war on Germany. Golf, and those days of innocence, came abruptly to an end and would never be quite the same again.

The two young men in the bottom match epitomised the contrasting fortunes of many in that dreadful, fateful war. Oxford's Henry Stokoe, soon after war broke out, applied for a commission. He went to the front, to Ypres, with his Battalion in May 1915. By September he was in command of a company which had lost all of its officers. His company fought hard under his leadership to hold first-line trenches at Hooge amidst heavy bombardment. But sadly one month later he was dead, killed accidentally by the premature explosion of a rifle grenade. He is buried in a small cemetery near Ypres. He was 21.

Cambridge's Oliver Lyttelton also signed up at the outbreak of war. As a Grenadier Guard, he was sent to France in February 1915. He served on the Western Front and survived, reaching the rank of major and was awarded the Military Cross. After the War he went into business, eventually becoming

[59] As will be recalled, the 1881 match did not take place due to bad weather.
[60] David Ryan played for Cambridge in the 2016 Varsity match having captained Oxford the previous year.

managing director of the British Metal Corporation. He then pursued a political career become the Conservative MP for Aldershot in 1940. During the Second World War, Churchill appointed him as the President of the Board of Trade and he sat in the War Cabinet where he held the post of Minister of State for War Production from 1942-45. He was subsequently elevated to the peerage becoming the 1st Viscount Chandos in 1954. From 1962-71 he was the first Chairman of the National Theatre. The Lyttelton Theatre, part of the National's South Bank complex, is named after him. He died in 1972 at the age of 79.

1915-19

The end was nigh also for the golf course at Whitwell Hill. The plague of worms 'whose natural nesting place seems to be on golf greens' continued to be a problem. In 1912, the hon sec, Charles Pigg, stated that receipts had shown a considerable falling off. Even if war had not come along, it is doubtful if the course would have survived much longer. But finally in October 1915 with so few players in residence, it was decided at a general meeting of the club to close the course at Coton and terminate the leases at the earliest possible date.

It is hard to make a judgement on how good a course Whitwell Hill was. No matches were ever played there against other clubs or societies (due to the arrangement with Worlington), so we have no independent critiques. Darwin was sceptical of its qualities:

> *Before the War the CUGC had its home at some meadows at Coton, which had certainly more attractive surroundings but were otherwise as muddy and dull as ever Coldham was.*

But it should be recorded for posterity that it was a course first marked out by Willie Park Jr, with greens and tees created by Willie Duncan (who marked out the original Old Course at the Gogs) and with much of the bunkering and other course changes due to Harry S Colt. It may have been an uninspiring piece of land to play golf upon, but it would not usurp Coldham Common of its title as the worst golf course ever.

In May 1917, the end finally came. The two colleges who owned the land, King's and Clare, received letters from the Cambridge War Agricultural Committee stating:

> *My Committee consider that it is in the National Interest that the whole of the land recently occupied by the University Golf Club should be broken up without delay for cropping in 1918.*

And that is how it remains to this day. The photograph shows the land today where the Whitwell Hill course was laid out for twelve years from 1902 to 1914. It consists of several arable fields, one of which is on a quite steep incline; the roofs of the colleges can be seen in the distance.

When the War ended, there was no desire to recreate the golf course. In 1921, the pavilion, which had been constructed in 1905, was removed to the site of the new King's and Clare cricket ground on Barton Road. In December 1922, the rites were completed when the Ministry of Agriculture settled the colleges' claims for compensation for the use of Whitwell Hill with a cheque for £173, with £77 allotted to Kings and £96 to Clare. It was all over.

The site of the CUGC golf course at Whitwell Hill near Coton, 2016.

10

Four epilogues

What Linskill did next

Linskill had laid down significant roots in St Andrews well before he moved there permanently with his wife, Jessie, and two daughters, Violet and Nora, in 1896. He had been a member of the R&A since 1875. He probably met his wife-to-be there around 1880. And, he played golf there every summer from June until September. An early address that we have for him is 17 Pilmour Links, a few doors down from Old Tom Morris's workshop; and from 1899 until his death in 1929, his home with his family was 17 Murray Park.

A sketch of 'Tommy' Linskill on R&A headed notepaper, 1895.

Linskill's larger-than-life personna in St Andrews resulted in him being caricatured in two novels; as 'the man with the "spats"' in Horace Hutchinson's *Bert Edward The Golf Caddie*; and as Twinkle in *The Haunted Major* by Robert Marshall.

Rather surprisingly, it seems that his interest in playing golf waned somewhat upon taking up permanent residency in St Andrews. Throughout his life, Linskill assiduously maintained scrapbooks. Five of these reside in the *Special Collections* at St Andrews University and two more are held by the R&A. Within these, only one newspaper clipping was uncovered that referred to his own golf after 1896:

> *Mr W T Linskill … does not play much golf nowadays, but I am told that his skill with the putter is as great as ever. A few years ago Mr Linskill was brought*

back into the golfing arena to play with a partnerless aspirant for the medal. He had never till that day played with a rubber-cored ball, yet on the first green he lipped the hole at a distance of twenty yards, and is reported to have declared with emphasis that had the ball been a gutty he would certainly have holed it.

There was no date on the clipping but presumably it was sometime after 1902 when the Haskell golf ball was introduced and replaced gutta percha.

There is no record of Linskill participating in any matches for the Oxford and Cambridge Golfing Society which was formed in 1898. It is without question that he would have been invited to join, given that the first president of the Society was Horace Hutchinson who fully acknowledged that Linskill was the prime mover in organising the first Varsity match in 1878, and the first captain was his very good friend, John Low. Either the matches played were too far away from St Andrews for him to travel to, or he no longer felt able to play golf to a sufficient standard to be involved.

Towards the end of his life, Linskill was interviewed by H V Morton and appears in his engaging travel book, *In Search of Scotland*, published in 1929. Linskill had this to say about golf at that time; he also reminisced about golf in the days of his youth:

> *Golf today … is a ladies' game compared with the golf I remember at St Andrews half a century ago. I remember playing with hand-hammered gutta-percha balls. Damned annoying things when they broke! The rule in those days was that you put the new ball on the place where the largest fragment of the old one fell! … By gad, sir, in those days the daisies were so thick at St Andrews that we never played a white ball! I remember how the caddies used to say: "Red or yellow ball, sir!" And, by Jove – the moonlight games! How dashed well I remember playing when the moon was full, with 'fore caddies to tell us where the ball had gone, and a fellow following behind with a wheelbarrow full of refreshments! Those were the days, my boy!*

With golf playing a less prominent role in his life, his other interests had room to flourish.

Following in his father's footsteps, he got involved in civic life. His father, Captain Linskill, had been the first mayor of Tynemouth in 1849. Shortly after settling in St Andrews, W T Linskill became a town councillor. Initially he sat on the lighting and paving committees. He was particularly scathing about the poor quality of street lighting in St Andrews even before he became a councillor as the following letter attests:

> *I have written in the St Andrews Citizen about the lamps until I got as sick of writing as people must have got of reading … What is wanted is more lamps, the lamps left lighted all night, and proper lighting rods procured … It will never do for St Andrews to be so far behind the times ….*

In due course he became the Dean of Guild, responsible for building regulations in the town. Thereafter in St Andrews he was known as Dean Linskill, retaining that position for a quarter of a century until near the end of his life. As well as sorting out the town's lighting he was also active in keeping the equipment of the fire brigade up-to-date, as the cartoon below illustrates. Throughout his lengthy tenure he was acknowledged to have given good service to the town and was a popular councillor.

A cartoon from a St Andrews newspaper showing W T Linskill and the local firemen.

Another contribution he made to St Andrews' life was in the theatrical arts. Following on from the interest he had developed while at Cambridge, he produced and acted in numerous plays and pantomimes in St Andrews. He seemed particularly interested in burlesque. Two productions he put on were

Whittington and His Cat and Aladdin and the Wonderful Lamp. He also arranged musical evenings, typically to raise funds for good causes such as the local lifeboat. His musical interests also had an outlet via his civic role. He was responsible for arranging summer outdoor entertainments for the townsfolk and visitors. He was a particular advocate of Pierrot troupes – travelling seaside shows – typically composed of song and dance, comedy and juggling.

If that was not enough, he was also a founder member in 1903, and subsequently the longstanding president of the St Andrews Antiquarian Society. The society was not a forum for romantics and cranks. A number of major figures in St Andrews were members: Dr James Younger, a wealthy philanthropist of the Younger's brewing family; James Baxter, who would become the Professor of Ecclesiastical History at St Andrews from 1922-70; and James Irvine, who would be knighted and become the Principal of the University from 1921-52.

Linskill's interest in all matters antiquarian stemmed from travels he undertook as a younger man. Apparently he had travelled a good deal 'on the Continent' and, being interested in religious affairs, he visited many of the famous European cathedrals where 'church crypts and subterranean passages appealed to the romantic side of his nature'. He was particularly fascinated by catacombs and underground passages that he had seen in Rome, Naples, Syracuse, Venice and Maastricht and 'many places in old days which were similarly situated as St Andrews was'.

In due course, Linskill would carry out many explorations of the town's ancient sites. He strongly believed in the existence of a labyrinth of subterranean passages under St Andrews, possibly with treasure hidden within. However, he never managed to find any. He got extremely excited on one occasion on discovering a tunnel under the road near the Pends[61] which led to the cathedral. It was subsequently determined to be a large medieval sewage pipe.

A cartoon of Linskill in Pierrot outfit, golf club in hand, in search of subterranean passages.

[61] A mid-fourteenth century large stone gatehouse.

123

To the end of his days he believed that there existed a secret 'wee stairway' from the cathedral down into the underground passages. Unfortunately he never did find it and, if it exists, it remains hidden to this day.

So, there we have it. His was a life lived to the full with golf, musical theatre, high church, civic duty and antiquarianism, and all written about exhaustively in articles and letters to the newspapers throughout. More than enough for any man, you would think. And yet, there was one more abiding interest in Linskill's life, and it is probably the one for which he is most commonly associated with to this day – the collecting and telling of St Andrews' ghost stories!

His fascination in the myths and legends of the ancient town must have come early in his life. It is easy to see how a staunchly religious man with interests in historic relics and the lives and ways of the ancients could be drawn to tales of phantoms, apparitions and other ghostly figures. Maybe his narrow avoidance of death in the Tay Bridge disaster further caused him to contemplate life beyond the grave. Whatever the cause, he became enthralled with the supernatural and began collecting traditional tales about ghosts. He had some of them printed in the local papers and then, in 1911, he published his book, *St Andrews Ghost Stories*. It was a great success and long-lived, remaining in print for over sixty years.

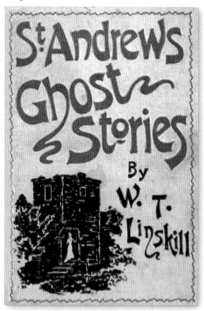

Front cover of Linskill's St Andrews Ghost Stories, 1911.

Not only did the book sell well with its tales of the Veiled Nun, the White Lady of the Haunted Tower and the Screaming Skull of Greyfriars, but Linskill dined out on the stories giving after-dinner speeches and even organised ghost tours of St Andrews. His booming voice and theatrical manner brought the stories to life. In a way they brought Linskill to life too.

However, there was an admission. He never personally encountered a ghost in his entire life, despite many attempts to do so. Rather than conclude from this lack of experiential evidence that they did not exist, Linskill simply attributed this to he himself not being sufficiently psychic. To the believer deeply embedded within him, it was quite simply the only explanation.

When H V Morton travelled to St Andrews, he was encouraged to seek out 'old Linskill [because] he knows more about St Andrews than the rest of us put together'. Morton met him in 1929 only a few months before he would die, and this is what he had to say about him:

> *I found the ghost-hunter looking remarkably like a possibly violent retired major-general. My first feeling was one of pity for the ghost who attempts to haunt him. An enormous voice, a baggy suit of plus fours, a pipe, a drooping grey moustache, a pair of eyes which have not altered since he was thirty. Here were seventy-four years carried with the gallantry of fifty. He looked as though his life had agreed with him like a good dinner ... .*

> *Mr Linskill is a great possession for any town, and a still greater one for any publisher who could get a book out of him. Seventy-four years have never sat more lightly on a man, and, in spite of his youthfulness, he is refreshingly of an older and a happier age: the age of squires and 'Johnnies', horses and fine manners, and men who really did, when worked up, say "Zounds, sir!"*

All in all, a privileged life well lived.

Coldham's Common after golf

Any signs that a golf course had existed on Coldham's Common for a quarter of a century must have disappeared fairly quickly after it was abandoned in May 1902. No bunkers were ever constructed to provide a ghostly reminder of what had once been there. The tees and greens, which were essentially closely mown and rolled areas, simply returned to the way that nature had intended. Life on Coldham's Common more or less reverted to how it had been before Linskill came up with the idea of creating a golf course there.

The Commons' committee minute book on 6 September 1901 notes that it was planned to plant some clumps of trees on Coldham's, perhaps to take away a little of the bareness of the landscape. Otherwise the annual cycle of the cattle arriving for pasture during the summer months continued, as it does even to this day.

During the Great War, the rifle range saw increased activity. It was used to train the troops who would be sent to fight, whilst the common itself was used as a camp for soldiers on their way to the battlefields of Europe. Volunteer groups who had practised their shooting skills on this spot for many years would form the 1st Battalion, The Cambridgeshire Regiment. As well as the main rifle range and butts, a miniature rifle range and butts, for small arms practice, was also created in the area between the GER line and Coldham's Lane. The drains laid in this area by CUGC in the 1890s to reduce the waterlogging must have helped. The main rifle butts on Coldham's Common are still there today. It is a sizeable chalk mound, purportedly the third highest point in Cambridge. No wonder the GER had to pay the town corporation £1500 to move the butts in 1895.

In the 1930s, and then again in the 1950s, the expansion of Cambridge resulted in much new housing being built in the vicinity of the common. The Coldham's Common which once sat on the periphery of Cambridge, and was mostly surrounded by fields, gradually became absorbed into what it is today, an important green open space in the midst of an urban landscape.

The cattle grazing on Coldham's Common, June 2015.

The rifle butts on Coldham's Common, 2016.

Sports amenities were created. A football team, Abbey United, was founded in 1912 and in 1951 became Cambridge United, playing its matches at the Abbey Stadium which overlooks the common on the north side near Newmarket Road. The open air bathing pools of the Victorian era became the indoor Abbey Swimming Pool and now the Abbey Leisure Complex. There may no longer be golf on Coldham's Common, but many other sports utilise the space which now includes football pitches and a floodlit all-weather sports area. There is even an American Football team based there.

Some areas of the common are classed as a local nature reserve, particularly at the east end where golf holes once existed, and are managed to encourage plant and grassland biodiversity, creating a habitat for wildlife. Kingfishers and water voles are occasionally spotted in Coldham's Brook and the various man-made ditches around the common. It is recognised as an important amenity to the local community. However few, if any, are aware that it was once a golf course where hundreds of young gentlemen in red jackets enjoyed serious fun for a quarter of a century.

There is one important edifice from the days of golf on Coldham Common that needs to be mentioned – the clubhouse. As was explained at the end of Chapter 8, the pavilion and the house where the professional lived were sold off in October 1902. The site was purchased by a company which established the Coldham Model Laundry. Although there are some reports of changes in ownership during the First World War, it seems that it remained as an operational laundry until at least the 1950s. The photograph shows an aerial view of the former clubhouse further developed as the laundry in 1928. The railway crossing on Coldham's Road (visible in the bottom left hand corner of the photograph) is still called Laundry Lane Crossing to this day.

Coldham Model Laundry, 1928.

This stretch of land adjacent to Coldham's Road was eventually developed into a small industrial park housing light manufacturing and service companies. The author assumed that the clubhouse-cum-laundry would have been cleared away many years ago to be replaced by more modern buildings. Amazingly this turned out not to be the case. The photograph below shows an aerial view taken from *Google Earth* of the site where the clubhouse resided – the roofs of the pavilion and the professional's house are clearly visible. It is still there today!

A site visit revealed that, although in a rather dilapidated state, the buildings were still in use as part of the warehouse facility of the Belfast Bed Superstore, 125 years after they were erected. The current owners knew that it had been a laundry in the past but were quite surprised to be told that it was the University golf clubhouse prior to that.

Aerial view of remains of the golf clubhouse, 2015.

The remains of the Coldham professional's house, 2016.

The remains of the Coldham clubhouse, 2016.

The final words on Coldham Common should quite rightly go to Bernard Darwin. One of his earliest anthologies, *Tee shots and Others* (1911), consisted mostly of articles previously printed in *The Evening Standard*. In it there is one article, *Pleasant Memories*, that contains this reminiscence about Coldham Common:

> It is indeed rather curious that the courses over which we grow most sentimental are not infrequently some of the worst in existence. There never was, I suppose, in point of general atrocity a course to compare with Coldham Common at Cambridge. Flatness and muddiness and caddies that were hooligans in embryo – these were its only characteristics, and yet I was fond of it. I am fond of it even now, when I see it a derelict wilderness of grass with what was once the clubhouse, converted into a laundry – surely the only link that ever existed between cleanliness and Coldham.

Coldham's Common with buttercups in full bloom, June 2016.

The search for the Linskill Cup

The Linskill Cup is an iconic trophy. It harks back to a time when golf was only beginning to find its feet in nineteenth-century England. For a quarter of a century it was the major scratch prize of the Cambridge University Golf Club at Coldham Common. Some of the winners would go on to become renowned golfers of that era; others would not be heard of again. The winning scores were sometimes over 100 and on a few occasions astonishingly low. It was usually played for three times a year (once per term). Rarely did rain, wind or even snow in the winter months stop the competitions from going ahead; only the long grass on the common in May sometimes defeated them.

When golf was finally abandoned at Coldham Common in 1902, the Linskill Cup continued to be played for at the new course created by CUGC near Coton, on the outskirts of Cambridge. After this course was ploughed up during the First World War, Royal Worlington and Newmarket became the club's home and competition for the Linskill Cup carried on there, albeit less frequently. Perhaps because some other more lustrous trophies were donated to CUGC over time, the Linskill Cup began to lose its sheen. Maybe also the awareness of its distinguished past dimmed. The last recorded competition for the trophy was in 1977, a century after it had all begun.

The Linskill Cup has gone missing on a number of occasions, sometimes lost for years until rediscovered by chance or as a result of enquiries and investigation. In 2015, when the President of CUGC, Professor Adrian Dixon, kindly showed me the trophies held by the club at that time, I realised that the Linskill Cup was not amongst them, and no-one currently associated with the club knew about it. So, it seemed that the Linskill Cup had disappeared once more.

The following tells the story of the Linskill Cup and the latter-day search for it. It is a fascinating tale with twists and turns, of heroes and possibly a rascal or two. The investigation drew on clues found in the CUGC minute books, conversations with old Blues and quite a bit of detective work in the hope that its whereabouts could be discovered and that the Linskill Cup could be returned to its rightful home again.

How it all began

As related earlier in the book, the Linskill Challenge Cup, as it was originally called, was donated in 1877 to the Cambridge University Golf Club by William T Linskill's father, Captain William Linskill, when the Linskill-inspired club had only been going for about a year. Given that there were only a dozen golf clubs in existence in England at that time, this would make it one of the oldest golf trophies in the country.

It was first played for on Wednesday 14 March 1877 and was reported upon in *The Field*. The first winner was Charles H Spence (Trinity) with a scratch score of 104. His winning score probably says more about the quality of the course at Coldham Common than about his standard of golf, for he played in the first three Varsity matches, winning one, halving one and losing the other.

As can be seen in the old photograph below, the Linskill Cup is a tankard with two handles, a loving cup in fact. According to Bernard Darwin it originally had a 'curious funnel-shaped leather cover' with the names of the winners written in gold letters upon it.

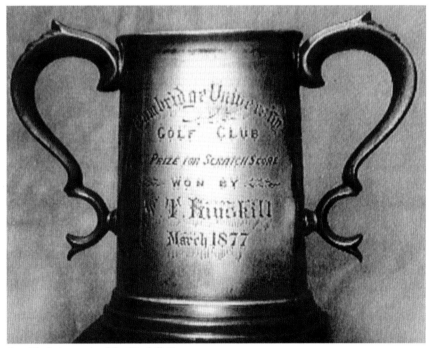

An old photograph of the Linskill Cup.

And now we come to the first piece of intrigue. As can be seen in the photograph, the wording etched upon the Cup says: 'Prize for Scratch Score; Won by W T Linskill, March 1877'. This is very odd since the article in *The Field* announced Spence as the winner with Linskill and P R Don tied second, four shots adrift. A possible, albeit questionable, explanation could be construed from an article in *The Field* a week later. This reported on a number of matches for the 'championship of the Green' where the holder was challenged. In the first match reported, Mr Spence, 'winner of the Linskill challenge cup', beat Mr Don; then Linskill challenged Spence and beat him. However, very shortly after that Mr Don challenged Linskill and won. If these challenge matches resulted in the Linskill Challenge Cup changing hands then Linskill indeed would have held it, albeit briefly, in March 1877. All that can be said is that it is a rather tenuous explanation.

The Linskill Cup at Coldham Common

On 26 May 1877, the terminal competition in the Easter term was held. C H Spence won the Linskill Cup again, this time with a score of 108. By trawling through *The Field* (weekly), *The Cambridge Review* (weekly in term time) and the CUGC minute books, it has been possible to construct an 'honours board' for the Linskill Cup while it was held at Coldham Common. Appendix I contains two tables of the known winners, one for the era from 1877-1889, when the nine-hole course was in use and the other from 1889-1902, when the eighteen-hole course was in use.

Of a possible 38 competitions between 1877-1889 (see Appendix I), a clear winner was identified on 31 occasions; there was a tie on two occasions but it is not known if a play-off took place or not; on one occasion (Easter term 1886) it was reported that there was no competition owing to the grass on the Common being too long at that time of year; and on the four other occasions no report of the competition appeared (three out of four of these were in the Easter term, so maybe the long grass defeated them then also).

Multiple winners during this period included: C H Spence (3), F G H Pattison (3), H B Boyd (4) and J C Wilson (5). Pattison, who like Spence, played off scratch, won in 1878 with the highest winning score from this era, 109. In an article written in *The Cambridge Review* by Bernard Darwin in 1923 about the Linskill Cup, he was curious about this:

> *There may appear nothing very remarkable about that [score]. People did not play very well about 1878, the golfer of today may say, and often took over a hundred. But if that scornful golfer will look at the history of the University match, he will observe that the same Mr Pattison played twice against Mr Horace Hutchinson. Once he beat him by five holes and once they halved .... . It is a lesson to those who play with rubber cored balls on beautifully kept courses not to judge their predecessors by their scores nor yet too scornfully.*

Horace Hutchinson would go on to win the Amateur Championship in 1886 and 1887. Pattison, a Scot who apparently learned his golf at Musselburgh, emigrated to Canada and there are no records of him playing golf again.

However, the outstanding player of this generation at Cambridge was undoubtedly William Welsh. He won the Linskill Cup eight times, including six in a row. The average score to win the Linskill Cup during this era (twice around the 9-hole course) was 95; Welsh won it in 1880 with 84, a truly remarkable score at that time. As noted in Chapter 5, the Welsh Cup which was donated to CUGC in 1929 in commemoration of him remains in the possession of the club to this day.

From 1889, competition for the trophy took place on the 18-hole course and a number of well-known players won the Linskill Cup between this time and 1902 (see Appendix 1). On three occasions, Harry Colt tied for first place; he won one play-off but the results of the other two were not reported (if they took place). The great John Low won twice, as did C E Hambro, P W Leathart, A C Lawrence and W G Howarth. However the dominant player of this era was undoubtedly Bernard Darwin who won on five out of the six occasions in which he participated.

The scores on the 18-hole course were much improved over the earlier 9-hole course (maybe the golfers were better too). There were eight winning scores in the 70s, including two 76s by Darwin. In the 1920s, Darwin wrote of his pride at having his name on the cup cover:

> *... with those golden letters belong to the days of Coldham Common, red coats with light blue collars and other things that have vanished.*

Lost and found

After Coldham Common was abandoned in 1902, the Linskill Cup was played for at the new course at Coton. Records for this period, from 1902-1914 are patchy with only 10 winners reported out of a possible 24 occasions in which the Cup might have been played (i.e. twice a year, in the Michaelmas and Lent terms). This was either because the hon sec, Charles Pigg, was less diligent in filing reports of results to the press than Linskill was, or that play for the Cup was more sporadic due to weather and course conditions at Whitwell Hill. Whitwell Hill was turned over to agriculture during the First World War and never re-opened.

During the First World War, the Linskill Cup went missing. On 7 February 1922, it was reported in *The Cambridge Review* that the Linskill Cup had recently been played for at the Gog Magog golf club, but in name only. W H Aiken won with 76. Of more significance was the following:

> *There are still no signs of either the [Linskill] Cup or [Pirie] Memento being found, all trace of them having been lost during the war. It therefore seems that it is almost time to cease holding this competition; and if they turn up later the winners' names for the past three years can be inscribed on them, and the competition restarted.*

It seemed that might be the end of it. However, a year later, on 19 February 1923, the following appeared in the CUGC minutes:

> *The Linskill Cup which had been missing for eight years was found on the day of the meeting. It was decided unanimously that the cup should be played for as the University scratch prize as before, and that the competition take place on the Royal Worlington and Newmarket golf course.*

This was such an exciting development that when he heard about it Darwin was drawn to write a full page article in *The Cambridge Review* on 6 June 1923 titled, 'The Finding of the Linskill Cup'. He opened with the following:

> *There is nothing more romantic than the finding of a lost treasure, and to the breasts of Cambridge golfers, of an older generation at any rate, the finding last term of the lost Linskill Cup brought a delightful and sentimental thrill. In itself the Cup enjoys a venerable place among golfing trophies for it dates back to 1878 [sic], and there are comparatively few prizes in any English club as old as that. It commemorates the name of a great character in the annals of the CUGC, Mr W T Linskill, who was for innumerable years Secretary to the club, and its curious funnel-shaped leather cover, with its record of the winners from earliest times, is an epitome of Cambridge golf.*

He then went on to describe how it was found again:

> *The circumstances of the losing and finding of the Cup appear to have been, as far as I understand them, full of mystery and romance. The captain of the Cambridge side flew to arms when war broke out, and his last words to his faithful gyp, as he buckled on his armour, were to take care of the Linskill Cup. The gyp was perfectly faithful but not, as it would seem of an enquiring turn of mind. He did not discover till this year that golf had begun again in Cambridge. He had, however, a friend, by trade a cabman, who mixed more with the world and kept up to date. The cabman knew the name of the captain of the golf club, and so the cup left the gyp's dark cupboard, and when last term the Cambridge side and the Oxford and Cambridge Golf Society dined together at the Pitt Club, it sat on the table in front of the Captain winking and blinking happily in the light.*

Darwin finished his piece with the hope that 'the Linskill Cup may now be treasured safely for ever'. Sadly this was not to be the case.

Henry Longhurst, shooting a 74, won the Linskill Cup at Worlington on 30 October 1929. Interestingly a year later, as the Linskill Cup was about to be played for again, the CUGC minutes dated 15 October 1930 noted that 'the whereabouts of the Linskill Cup was unknown'. An update appeared on 29 October 1930:

> *It is proposed that all cups should be insured, and since the last meeting the Secretary has endeavoured to trace the whereabouts of the Linskill Cup, and as far as could be discovered, it was in Canada.*

It could be inferred that the previous winner (i.e. Longhurst) might have had something to do with the Linskill Cup's trip abroad. In fact, in his autobiography, *My Life and Soft Times* (1971), Longhurst described a memorable trip taken in the summer of 1930 by ten members of CUGC to America. They travelled by ship and played around twenty clubs in the eastern USA. There is no mention of a match against a Canadian club but otherwise the story seems to fit. Interestingly this was during prohibition. Longhurst referred to illegal alcohol being provided by their hosts while on their tour, so maybe the Linskill Cup was used for that purpose. In any case, in November 1930, while the Cup was still apparently overseas, Longhurst won it again to retain it.

It continued to be played for but it seems that it took some time for the cup to be repatriated, because it was not until 15 May 1935 that the following update appeared in the CUGC minutes:

> *Mr Knox-Smith [honorary treasurer] thought that the Linskill Cup, now that it had been found again, should have the names of recent winners engraved upon it.*

Under lock and key

The Linskill Cup in subsequent years was played for annually at Worlington. It was even played for during the Second World War, D F Ashton winning it in 1942-43.

After the various disappearances of the cup, it seems that the club's trophies were retained over a lengthy period of time by the Cambridge jewellers, Munsey & Co, for prudent safekeeping. In 1956 the hon sec, W M Grindrod (Clare), complained that the CUGC cups were never seen by the winners of them and so the committee agreed that the cups could be taken out and kept in the winners' rooms provided that the secretary ensured that they were returned to Munsey's at the end of each term.

In 1959 the minutes noted that Mr Henry Longhurst wished to donate to CUGC a pewter tankard that he had acquired. It was agreed that this would be held by the Linskill Cup winner. It slightly suggests mea culpa on Longhurst's part in the Linskill Cup's disappearance in 1930.

During the 1960s and early 1970s the Linskill Cup was played for (or reported on) only sporadically. The only winners noted in the CUGC minutes during this period were:

1960-61: L G B Williamson (Corpus)
1961-62: P R Johnston (Queens')
1975-76: N J Grant (Christ's)
1976-77: A Evans-Pritchard (Trinity)

A number of old Blues from this era were contacted to see if they recalled seeing the Linskill Cup. Few had any memory of it. It would seem that the club's trophies had remained locked away for safekeeping, perhaps only put on display on special occasions, such as at club dinners. The last reported win, by Ambrose Evans-Pritchard, was forty years ago. There were no further references to it being played for in ensuing years and no-one now seemed to know of its whereabouts. It could not have disappeared into thin air, so there was a mystery to be solved.

The search begins

The search started in Cambridge. It seemed possible, as had happened during the First World War, that the Linskill Cup had simply been put somewhere for safekeeping and then forgotten about. With the honorary secretary typically holding the post for one year only, and if the CUGC minutes were not recorded diligently, such a thing could happen.

Munsey's, the jewellers, where the CUGC trophies had been held in the safe since the disappearance of the Linskill Cup in the 1930s was an obvious starting point. However, this did not progress far. Munsey's was no longer in business, having been taken over at some point in the past by Northern Goldsmiths.[62] Its premises at 17 Market Hill was now the outlet of another jeweller store, Mappin & Webb.[63]

The other possibility was that it had been stowed away in one of the colleges. But which one? There are thirty-one of them. Since the trophies retained by the club today are currently under lock and key at Peterhouse where Adrian Dixon was Master, perhaps a past CUGC President had taken on a similar responsibility.

[62]Subsequently re-named Goldsmiths.
[63]Mappin & Webb is also owned by Goldsmiths, which was subsequently re-named Aurum Holdings.

The most likely candidate was Sir Gordon Sutherland who was CUGC President from 1967-80 and was also Master of Emmanuel at the time when the Linskill Cup was last played for. There was further support for this possibility when some comments were discovered in the CUGC minutes from the mid-1970s about the safekeeping of the club's trophies. On 4 March 1974, at the CUGC AGM, it was minuted that:

> *The Captain pointed out that he had a request from Munzies (sic) that the Club's Cups (Ewen, Carr and Dunedin) which had been kept in Munzies safe without charge, should be removed. It would be necessary to find a new home for these and the President promised to look into the possibility of keeping them in Emmanuel.*

The minutes for the following year's AGM on 3 March 1975 noted:

> *The President said that the Cups of the Club now resided in the Buttery in Emmanuel.*

The Librarian at Pembroke, where the CUGC minute books are currently held, provided further encouragement for this line of enquiry when she mentioned that she had seen a large display cabinet at Emmanuel containing 'all sorts of interesting cups and trophies'.

With some excitement, I contacted Emmanuel. The following reply was received a few days later:

> *Dear Dr Morrison,*
>
> *Thank you for your enquiry, which has been passed on to the Archives. I have looked into this matter and am afraid I can only give a negative response. There is no mention of the golf trophies in either the Governing Body minutes or the papers of the committee that deals with College plate, nor is there anything about them in Sir Gordon Sutherland's correspondence files, and, last but not least, no CUGC trophies are listed in the College's inventory of plate. I think the cabinet [the Pembroke Librarian] referred to must be one of the display cases in the College Museum; there are several of these and some do indeed contain sporting cups, but they are all College, not University trophies and virtually all of them are Emmanuel Boat Club prizes.*
>
> *I do hope the trophies can be tracked down – but it does seem fairly certain that they did not come to Emmanuel.*
>
> *Best wishes*
>
> *Emmanuel College Archivist*

So, despite the CUGC minutes saying that the club's trophies were at Emmanuel in 1975, the college had no record of them ever being there. It was the end of that line of enquiry. Some other colleges were contacted, more in hope than expectation. But correspondence with King's, Jesus, Pembroke and Trinity all drew blanks. Perhaps this search for the Linskill Cup was going to end unfulfilled.

A breakthrough

The CUGC minutes are held in two large tomes, mostly hand-written by past honorary secretaries. The older of the two covers the period from 1889 until near the end of the Second World War; the newer one records the minutes from then onwards until the 1990s.[64] Given the focus of this book, I had mostly concentrated on the minutes for the early years, from 1889 until the commencement of the First World War. I had merely skim-read the minutes thereafter.

The CUGC minute books.

With the draft of the book nearing completion, I decided to re-read the early minutes to ensure that I had not missed anything material. Out of interest, I also decided to read both tomes cover-to-cover so that I would have a comprehensive understanding of the entire CUGC history. It was also possible, I hoped, that some interesting snippets might turn up.

---

[64]Subsequent minutes to date are retained on computer.

I was nearing the end of this read-through when I came across, almost as an aside, the following brief entry in 1988:

> *The win against Notts GC [on 5 March 1988] was the first Cambridge win*
> *at Hollinwell since the Linskill Cup was presented as the winner's trophy*
> *12 years before. This cup was originally the prize for an 18-hole annual*
> *medal at Worlington.*

So, the Linskill Cup was not in Cambridge after all. It had gone to Hollinwell in Nottinghamshire in 1977 when it had become the designated trophy for the long-running match between the two clubs. Perhaps the honorary secretary in 1976 should have minuted this rather important decision. Fortunately in beating the Notts club for the first time in 1988, the secretary in that year thought it worthy of mention.

I read on. But with new honorary secretaries being appointed each year, the Linskill Cup seems to have been forgotten about yet again. But then five years later another brief entry appeared, recording the minutes of the AGM held on 15 June 1993:

> *It was noted that the whereabouts of the Linskill Cup was still a mystery. Mr*
> *Uzielli [the Captain] recollected seeing a Linskill Cup at Hollinwell Golf Club.*
> *It was agreed that the President [Professor Michael Powell] would investigate*
> *this matter.*

So, the cup was still at Hollinwell in the early 1990s. This time there was a follow-up in the CUGC minutes in matters arising at the following year's AGM on 15 June 1994:

> *It was reported that the Linskill Cup had been traced to Hollinwell Golf*
> *Club where it was annually competed for in the match between the club*
> *and CUGC. It was agreed to regard the cup as being 'on loan' to Hollinwell*
> *and not to insist on its return to Cambridge. However, Mr Murphy [Senior*
> *Treasurer] undertook to write to the Secretary of the Hollinwell Club to put*
> *that understanding 'on the record' and to ask whether the cup was*
> *adequately insured.*

That was twenty-two years ago. There were no further references to the Linskill Cup. In due course, the longstanding match against the Notts golf club disappeared from the fixture list and the Linskill Cup was quietly forgotten about.

So, was the Linskill Cup still at Hollinwell? In March 2016, I contacted the secretary/manager there. Martin Bonner MBE responded promptly. Yes, he knew of the Linskill Cup but did not have it at hand, nor was it in the club's trophy cabinet. Mr Bonner promised to contact the club historian to investigate. My heart sank. Had it gone missing yet again when it seemed to be just within grasp?

There was good news of sorts. He had a photograph of the Linskill Cup which appeared in the club's centenary book written in 1989 and he forwarded it to me. This is the old photograph shown earlier in this epilogue. The photograph also showed a base had been added to the cup during its time at Hollinwell. Upon the base the following inscription appeared:

> *W T Linskill has gone down to history as the founder of golf at Cambridge. This tankard, won by him in 1877, was discovered by chance at Hollinwell. At the suggestion of Henry Longhurst, who himself captained Cambridge in 1930/31, it was played for in the annual match between Cambridge University and Notts Golf Clubs in 1977, exactly a century after it was first won by Linskill.*

Once again we have the weaving together of the story of the Linskill Cup and a role played by Longhurst. There are certainly some questions that we would have liked to ask him. Why was the Linskill Cup at Hollinwell when it was 'discovered by chance'? When Longhurst donated a tankard in 1959, why did he choose to connect it with the Linskill Cup winner? How did it arise that Longhurst suggested that the Linskill Cup be played for between the two clubs? Sadly, these questions may have to remain unanswered as Longhurst died in 1978, one year after the two clubs began playing for the Cup.

A couple of months passed with no news from Hollinwell. The book was nearing completion and it increasingly looked likely that this chapter might have to end with the search for the Cup being unfulfilled. Then on 10 May 2016 a call came through from Martyn Bonner – the Linskill Cup had been found! A handyman at the club discovered it in the cellar. Apparently since it was no longer played for between the Notts club and CUGC it was no longer on display but had remained safely stowed away below decks.

Correspondence quickly took place between Adrian Dixon and Martin Bonner. It was agreed that since the Linskill Cup was no longer being played for between the two clubs, it should be returned to Cambridge. On 23 June, on behalf of CUGC, the author went to Hollinwell to collect the Linskill Cup. On arrival, it was sitting on the secretary's desk 'winking and blinking' awaiting its repatriation. I held it in both hands. It is six-and-a-half inches tall, made of pewter and has a glass bottom. Interestingly, it was made by Munsey & Co who had subsequently kept it in their safe from the 1930s until the 1970s. Sadly the 'curious funnel-shaped leather cover' with the winners' names inscribed, as described by Darwin, was not with it. So the cover's whereabouts remains a mystery. But the Cup, which had been away for four decades, was now returning to its *alma mater* one hundred and forty years after it had first been played for on the worst golf course ever at Coldham Common.

The mystery now solved and the cup returned, this would seem a fitting ending, but there was a final surprise in store. The photograph below shows the Linskill Cup at a slightly different angle to the older photograph shown earlier.

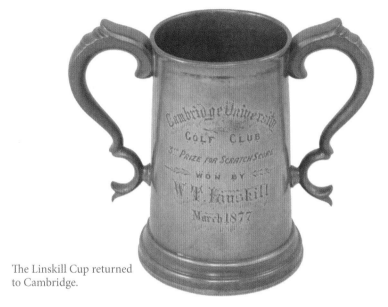

The Linskill Cup returned to Cambridge.

It can be seen that the wording on the Cup is not 'Prize for Scratch Score' but '3rd Prize for Scratch Score'! That at least partially squares with the facts reported earlier that C H Spence was the first winner of the Linskill Cup in March 1877. Let's return to the actual article that appeared in *The Field* on 17 March 1877:

> *The Cambridge University Golf Club held their terminal meeting on the links at Coldham Common, on Wednesday [14 March 1877]. The order for the different prizes was as follows: – C H Spence (Trinity), 104; W T Linskill and P R Don (Jesus), 108; Rev G Pirie (Queens'), 111 ... . The Linskill Challenge Cup and the first prize fell to Mr Spence. The Pirie Handicap Medal was tied for by Messrs Don and Linskill, and the tie will be played off today, the loser getting the second handicap prize.*

So, although it was reported that Linskill and Don had tied for second behind Spence, we must presume that Don won the play-off for the Pirie Handicap Medal and as a consequence Linskill was deemed to have come third (out of the fourteen entrants) in the scratch competition.

How odd that one of the oldest golf trophies in England commemorates the golfer who came third! But then, as we now know, nothing about Linskill was ever straightforward or without a hint of eccentricity.

The search for the Dunedin Cup

Andrew Graham Murray

As explained in Chapter 2, Andrew Graham Murray, as a twenty-year old Trinity undergraduate, was one of the founders of the Cambridge University Golf Club in 1869. After obtaining a 2nd class honours in classics in 1872, he went on to have a hugely successful legal and political career.

Following a brief period working in his father's practice, Tods Murray & Jamieson, he decided to pursue a career as an advocate. He was admitted to the Scottish bar in 1874 and, in due course, specialised in conveyancing and patent cases. Although not a great orator, he developed 'the gift of clear-headed, logical and lucid exposition'.[65] The year 1891 was momentous for Graham Murray. He became a Queen's Counsel, he was elected as the MP for Bute and then became the Solicitor-General for Scotland under Lord Salisbury's Conservative government. In 1896 he was promoted to Lord Advocate

Caricature of Andrew Graham Murray, the Lord Advocate, Vanity Fair, 22 October 1896.

---

[65]*Oxford Dictionary of National Biography*, www.oxforddnb.com

142

and became a privy councillor. In 1903 he became the Secretary for Scotland with a seat in Arthur Balfour's cabinet. Murray left the government and parliament in February 1905 on being appointed Lord Justice General and Lord President of the Court of Session in Edinburgh. He was raised to the peerage as Baron Dunedin[66] of Stenton in Perthshire on 9 March 1905. In 1913, Dunedin was chosen to fill one of the two new positions as a Lord of Appeal-in-Ordinary in the House of Lords, created to strengthen the supreme appeals court. He would remain in that position for the next nineteen years. During this tenure, he was created Viscount Dunedin of Stenton in 1926. He died in 1942 at the age of 92.

Despite his appetite for high office, it was not all work and no play. Graham Murray was steeped in golf throughout his life. As mentioned earlier, he became a member of the Honourable Company of Edinburgh Golfers in 1867, prior to going up to Cambridge and was elected as a member of the R&A in 1870 while he was still an undergraduate. In 1892 he received the ultimate accolade, becoming the captain of the R&A. It is perhaps less well-known that as the MP for Bute, he also captained the newly opened Rothesay golf club in the same year. He followed this in 1894 and 1895 by becoming the captain of the Honourable Company of Edinburgh Golfers which, a few years earlier, had moved from Musselburgh to its new course at Muirfield. When his political career took him to London, he became a member of Sunningdale and in the 1920s achieved the considerable honour of captaining that club on four occasions.

Lord Dunedin returns to Cambridge

And so, it is against this background that Lord Dunedin came to Cambridge on 16 June 1928 to give a speech at a dinner held in his honour by the committee of CUGC. We know this because a copy of it resides within the CUGC minute books. The bulk of his speech covered the fascinating account of getting golf going at Cambridge during his time there as an undergraduate and the formation of the club in 1869. While we also have the correspondence in *The Field* from George Gosset, the other key figure in the first club, Dunedin's speech both corroborates and enriches the story (as it is related in Chapter 2).

In the final part of his speech, he turned to some correspondence he had recently had with Claude Carnegie who, it will be recalled, was the first honorary secretary of the club. Specifically, he was the man who collected the half-crown subscriptions from the seventeen original members of the club nearly

---

[66]Dunedin derives from *Dùn Èideann*, the Gaelic name for Edinburgh.

sixty years before. Carnegie apparently held onto the subscription money, as Dunedin recounted:

> *I suggested interest, but he at once pleaded the Statute of Limitations. Then I asked him, had he got the original 2s/6ds, and he said that straitened circumstances had prevented that. However, he was quite willing to part with them and willing to do more: as he knew a Director of the Bank of England and thanks to him, and also what I did in London, we were able to get 17 half-crowns of dates prior to 1869, being the original number which were collected under the scheme of 1869.*

Lord Dunedin then proceeded to reveal a cup which he wished to donate to the club, encrusted with these seventeen half-crowns! He hoped that the club would accept it. He also created an inscription to go with it:

> *In memoriam primae Golfsocietatis Cantabrigienis nat. 1869 ob.s.p. 1871 hoc pocolum nummis contemporaneis ornatum donaverunt fundatores Vicecomes Dunedin at Carnegie e coll. s.s. Trin. Gosset e col. Regal. 1928 superstites.*

Roughly this translates as, 'In memory of the first Cambridge golf club, born 1869, died without issue 1871, this cup adorned with contemporary coins is bestowed by the surviving founders, Viscount Dunedin and Carnegie of Trinity College and Gosset of King's College, 1928.'

This provides us with the defining evidence, that the Cambridge University Golf Club can be dated back to 1869. At that time, the only other golf clubs in England were Royal Blackheath, Old Manchester (although possibly in abeyance at the time), Royal North Devon (Westward Ho!), London Scottish at Wimbledon Common, Royal Liverpool at Hoylake and Alnmouth on the Northumberland coast.

It is for this reason that, although the Dunedin Cup is not as old nor does it have the golfing pedigree of the Linskill Cup with its famous winners from the nineteenth century, there is a greater romance about it.

In closing, he said:

> *Well, I give you the Cup and the only stipulation I would like to make is that it is to be a Challenge Cup. I do not think it ought to be given to one player, for with its little history it belongs to the Club. As to where it is to be played for, whether it is to be by handicap or scratch, whether it is to be by holes or strokes, I leave that entirely to your own determination.*

The CUGC minutes of 18 October 1928 record that Lord Dunedin had kindly presented a Cup. It was resolved that it would be played for in a match-play knockout competition consisting of sixteen players[67] (with a qualifying round if necessary); that it would be called the Lord Dunedin Cup; that the entrance fee would be 2s/6d (how appropriate!); and that the winner would receive a replica of the Cup paid for out of the entrance money.

Reports on the Dunedin Cup

The Dunedin Cup, as it simply became known, was played for from 1929 onwards. The early winners received replicas, until these ran out in 1937, when it was decided not to make any more 'since there were no replicas for the other cups'.

The roll call of winners of the Dunedin Cup is patchy. The first victor is not known. There is some evidence that Henry Longhurst won the Dunedin Cup in 1931. The earliest actual report of the Dunedin Cup competition appeared in May 1932:

> *The University scratch Knock Out Competition was won by P F H White (Trinity Hall). The final was played at Mildenhall on May 7th, and White defeated K T Thomson (St Johns) by 3 and 2 over 36 holes .... The winner was three under fours for the 16 holes of the second round.*

Thereafter the minutes only report the following winners:

1934-35: P B Lucas (Pembroke)
1937-38: J D A Langley (Trinity)
1942-43: N G Darrah (Peterhouse)
1943-44: A A F Bryson (Pembroke)
1948-49: I H Stackhouse (Pembroke)
1960-61: L G B Williamson (Corpus) – score 70
1961-62: P R Johnson (Queens') – score 68

It can be seen that in the early 1960s, on the final two occasions when we have results recorded, it had changed format from matchplay to 18-hole medal play.

Why would such an illustrious trophy become rather peripheral within CUGC? It should be recalled that the Dunedin Cup was donated in 1928. Shortly thereafter, the club was in receipt of two other handsome trophies, the Welsh Cup in 1929 and the Carr Cup in 1930.[68] At that time, the Linskill Cup was also still being played for. It slightly suggests that there were simply too many cups. There was not sufficient time in the academic year to fit in so many competitions, especially

[67]Subsequently raised to thirty-two on 30 January 1929.
[68]See Appendix 4 for a brief history of these two trophies.

with a burgeoning fixture list of matches against prestigious clubs, which took up most weekends. Something had to give. And it seems that it was the Dunedin Cup.

Furthermore, following the Longhurst-inspired disappearance of the Linskill Cup to the Americas in 1930, the club rightly thought it best to keep its precious silverware under lock and key. Over many years, probably the only time that the members saw the club's trophies would be at important club dinners. Simply put, the Dunedin Cup was out of sight and out of mind.

As reported previously in the search for the Linskill Cup, the CUGC minutes in March 1974 noted that there had been a request from Munsey's to remove the club's trophies from its safe. The Dunedin Cup was specifically referred to in this context. The following year's minutes reported that the cups were now in Emmanuel College where the President of CUGC, Sir Gordon Sutherland, was the Master at that time. However as previously explained, the current archivist at Emmanuel could find no record of the CUGC silverware ever having been there. Unlike the Linskill Cup, there were no further references to the Dunedin Cup in the minutes after 1974. It has been missing ever since.

A search without clues

It was difficult to know where to start looking for the Dunedin Cup. Enquiries amongst old Blues produced no recollections of ever seeing the trophy. Even one of the winners whom I spoke with, did not remember it at all. It presumably remained in the safe even on competition days.

One line of thought was that it might have been decided to use the Dunedin Cup as a trophy to be played for in one of CUGC's major fixtures, like the Linskill Cup being adopted for the match against the Notts golf club. But which one? In 1974-75, the Blues participated in thirty-five fixtures. Even if all of those clubs and societies were contacted, it is doubtful that anyone today would recall a trophy being put up for matches which took place four decades ago.

However, a perusal of the 1974-75 fixture list identified one possible candidate – Sunningdale.

The cup presented by Lord Dunedin to Sunningdale GC, 1923.

After all, CUGC had been playing Sunningdale since 1903 when Harry Colt invited them to the then two-year old club. And, Lord Dunedin had been a member and the captain on four occasions in the 1920s. I contacted the club, explaining my search for the cup and its history. To my amazement, I received a reply saying that there was indeed a Dunedin Cup at Sunningdale! The reply also included a photograph of the cup.

Alas, it was not the CUGC Dunedin Cup. First, there were no half-crowns encrusted in the cup. And second, the inscription upon it said:

Presented to the Sunningdale Golf Club by the Captain, Lord Dunedin, on the opening of the New Course, Nov 1923.

Intriguingly, I subsequently discovered that this Dunedin Cup had also disappeared for a time. There are no recorded winners of the cup at Sunningdale between 1938 and 1951, although the Second World War may partly explain this. The trophy is still played for to this day in an 18-hole strokeplay competition under handicap.

By this point, I had begun to accept that finding the Dunedin Cup was going to be a step too far. My focus now was on completing the book and getting it ready for publication. In early September 2016, I was checking a few facts and working through a final list of relatively minor queries. One of these was to find out when Munsey's the jewellers, whose shop had been at 17 Market Hill, had been taken over by Goldsmiths. A web search did not shed any light on this. All that I was able to ascertain was that Mappin & Webb, which now had a store at this address, was part of the same group of companies. I decided to drop into the shop in the hope that someone might be able to help me with my query.

An opportunity arose on 7 September. When I arrived that morning both relatively young assistants in the store were busy with customers. However, a senior manager was called forth from the back office to deal with me. Mr Mark Cooper kindly listened while I explained that I was writing a book about the history of the Cambridge University Golf Club and the reason for my visit was to find out about Munsey's where the club's trophies had been kept in the safe from the 1930s until the 1970s. I was in luck – he was familiar with the history of Munsey's.

David Munsey, who was born in Willingham, Cambridgeshire in 1842, founded his jeweller and silversmith business around 1867 and is known to have had a shop on the market square in Cambridge from 1885. The current building where 17 Market Hill resides was built in the 1930s and it is believed that Munsey's moved a few doors down to this location at that time. However, by then it was no longer owned by David Munsey – he had sold the business to two brothers, Edwin and Leslie Jackson,[69] around 1901 (when Munsey would have been about sixty). Under the Jacksons' ownership it continued to trade under the name of Munsey's until the business was eventually sold in 1966 to Northern Goldsmiths. Even then, it continued to trade as Munsey's. It was only in the early 1990s that the shop was re-branded as Goldsmiths and then subsequently as Mappin & Webb around 2003.

Mr Cooper explained that he knew about this because he had been working in the store since 1978. Out of casual interest, I asked if he had any recollection of the golf trophies being kept in the safe. I told him that some had disappeared in the past, but that I had recently found one, the Linskill Cup, which coincidentally had been made by Munsey & Co around 1877. He said that over the years they had ended up with a number of old unclaimed sporting trophies. From time to time, they would contact the colleges but some remained unclaimed to this day. In fact, he said, they still had one without an inscription upon it, just a brown tag attached saying 'Golf Club'. My heart skipped a beat. Perhaps a little cautiously he asked if I had any photographs of the trophies that I was looking for. Regretfully I told him that I did not, but that there was one called the Dunedin Cup which was quite distinctive because it had seventeen half-crowns dating prior to 1869 encrusted in it. With just the slightest of pauses, he said, "Oh, that's the one we have downstairs".

In the two minutes that passed while he went to fetch it, I contemplated the improbability of finding the Dunedin Cup. What if I had not bothered following up on my minor query about Munsey's? What if I had spoken to one of the younger

The Dunedin Cup and lid with its encrusted half-crowns.

[69]Edwin Jackson would become the mayor of Cambridge in 1930-31. He was noted to be the Senior Partner of Messrs Munsey & Co at that time.

staff members present that day who might not have known about Munsey's? What if Mr Cooper had not been in the store that day, or even more likely, had left at some point in the last forty years to work elsewhere? At that point, he returned with the Dunedin Cup in his hands. It was undeniably recognisable, adorned with silver half-crowns – ten around the body of the cup and the other seven upon the lid. It was suddenly quite overwhelming.

The Latin epitaph prepared by Lord Dunedin, 'In memory of the first Cambridge golf club … ' is not inscribed upon the cup. Presumably there must have been a base with a plaque bearing the inscription which has got lost somewhere along the way. Perhaps if they had remained in tandem, someone at the jeweller's shop in years gone by might have translated it and figured out that it belonged to the university golf club?

A closer inspection of the Dunedin Cup reveals a number of fascinating things about it. It is solid silver, weighing 3 lbs (1.4 kg), and the hallmarks indicate that it was made in Birmingham in 1927, the year before Lord Dunedin presented it to the club. It is intricately made. The half-crowns are not merely adhered to the cup and lid, they are inset such that the obverse sides, showing 'young' Victoria's head, are visible on the outside and the reverse of each coin can be seen from the inside of the cup and lid. This even applies to the coin atop the lid; it is affixed via two pins allowing it to be rotated so that both sides of the coin can be observed! As well as looking aesthetically attractive compared with simply sticking the coins onto the cup, perhaps this method of encrusting also avoided criminal charges of defacing legal tender under the Currency and Bank Notes Act 1928? Lord Dunedin would have known.

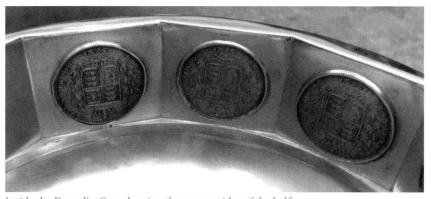

Inside the Dunedin Cup, showing the reverse sides of the half-crowns.

The half-crown atop the lid is also the oldest, dated 1840; the others date from 1842 to 1850. So, the coins were already around eighty years old when collected together by Lord Dunedin and Claude Carnegie. They seem to be in fine condition, so are probably quite valuable in their own right. It was curious that none of the half-crowns were dated around 1869, the year that the club was formed. However, research revealed that no half-crowns were issued between 1851 and 1873, the florin (two shillings) being used in its place during this period. A final surprise was found on the underside of the cup. It transpires that the cup had been made by a firm of silversmiths whose origins go back to Sheffield in 1775 and whose first store opened in Oxford Street in 1860. In the year prior to the Dunedin Cup's creation, they were responsible for making another golfing trophy, the Ryder Cup. Today, the firm is the custodian of the crown jewels. The makers of the Dunedin Cup were none other than Mappin & Webb!

Arrangements were quickly made between the President, Adrian Dixon, and Mappin & Webb to sort out any practicalities related to the return of the cup to CUGC. There might, for example, be the question of a few decades' worth of storage charges! On 23 September 2016, the President, with the author acting as minder, collected a beautifully cleaned-up Dunedin Cup. A short walk later and the cup which had been stowed in the safe for forty years only a few streets away, and which had barely been visible over the last eighty years, was returned to its rightful home, an exquisite memento commemorating the foundation in 1869 of the Cambridge University Golf Club.

The Dunedin Cup returned to CUGC.

Appendices

1. The Linskill Cup winners, 1877-1902

The first table below provides a record of the known Linskill Cup winners from 1877 to 1889 when the 9-hole course at Coldham Common was in use.

	Winner	College	Score	Comment
1876-77				
Michaelmas				
Lent	C H Spence	Trinity	104	First competition
Easter	C H Spence	Trinity	108	
1877-78				
Michaelmas	C H Spence	Trinity	95	
Lent	S G W Adams	Caius	100	
Easter	F G Pattison	Pembroke	109	
1878-79				
Michaelmas	F G H Pattison/ R C Faithfull	Pembroke/ Trinity	103	Play-off – result unknown
Lent	F G H Pattison	Pembroke	97	
Easter	No record			
1879-80				
Michaelmas	W Welsh	Jesus	98	
Lent	W Welsh	Jesus	95	
Easter	W Welsh	Jesus	84	
1880-81				
Michaelmas	W Welsh	Jesus	90	
Lent	W Welsh	Jesus	No record	
Easter	W Welsh	Jesus	No record	
1881-82				
Michaelmas	R C Faithfull	Trinity	101	
Lent	W Welsh	Jesus	96	
Easter	W Welsh	Jesus	No record	
1882-83				
Michaelmas	J L Casson	Trinity	92	W Welsh: 89, but did not enter
Lent	W T Linskill	Jesus	95	
Easter	No record	Jesus	No record	
1883-84				
Michaelmas	J C Wilson	Trinity	88	
Lent	J C Wilson	Trinity	89	
Easter	J C Wilson	Trinity	96	Beat H E B Peele in play-off

	Winner	College	Score	Comment
1884-85				
Michaelmas	J C Wilson	Trinity	94	
Lent	J C Wilson	Trinity	98	
Easter	No record			
1885-86				
Michaelmas	No record			
Lent	H B Boyd	Trinity Hall	86	
Easter	No competition			Grass too long
1886-87				
Michaelmas	H B Boyd	Trinity Hall	98	
Lent	H B Boyd	Trinity Hall	89	
Easter	H B Boyd	Trinity Hall	89	
1887-88				
Michaelmas	E Armitage	Trinity	86	
Lent	F N Fisher	Clare	105	
Easter	E Armitage	Trinity	93	
1888-89				
Michaelmas	C W Burn	Trinity	91	
Lent	C F Montgomery	Pembroke	97	
Easter	A Clark	Jesus	93	

The next table below provides a record of the known Linskill Cup winners from 1889 to 1902, the period when the 18-hole course was in use until Coldham Common was abandoned.

	Winner	College	Score	Comment
1889-90				
Michaelmas	H S Colt	Clare	90	Beat C F Montgomery in play-off
Lent	H S Colt/ N Hicks/ C F Montgomery	Clare/Trinity / Pembroke	95	Play-off result unknown
Easter	H S Colt/N Hicks	Clare/ Trinity	91	Play-off result unknown
1890-91				
Michaelmas	D A M Brown	Trinity Hall	84	
Lent	A M Joshua	Trinity	94	
Easter	R A Nicholson	Trinity	87	
1891-92				
Michaelmas	J L Low	Clare	86	
Lent	J L Low	Clare	79	
Easter	C E Hambro	Trinity	80	
1892-93				
Michaelmas	R A Nicholson	Trinity	83	
Lent	C E Hambro	Trinity	79	
Easter	A M Chance	Trinity	77	

	Winner	College	Score	Comment
1893-94				
Michaelmas	F R Upcher	Trinity Hall	87	
Lent	W T Linskill		85	Did not wish to accept the cup
Easter	No competition			Grass too long
1894-95				
Michaelmas	B Darwin	Trinity	85	
Lent	B Darwin	Trinity	92	
Easter	B Darwin	Trinity	83	
1895-96				
Michaelmas	B Darwin	Trinity	76	
Lent	J A Scott	Jesus	80	Note: B Darwin – 85
1896-97				
Michaelmas	B Darwin	Trinity	76	
Lent	B Darwin	Trinity	No record	
1897-98				
Michaelmas	A C Lawrence	Trinity Hall	77	
Lent	P W Leathart	Clare	79	
1898-99				
Michaelmas	P W Leathart	Clare	79	
Lent	A C Lawrence	Trinity Hall	82	
1899-1900				
Michaelmas	N F Hunter	Clare	83	
Lent	G H Hardie	Christ's	81	
1900-01				
Michaelmas	W G Howarth	King's	78	
Lent	W G Howarth	King's	82	Beat W T D Bodkin in play-off
1901-02				
Michaelmas	C B L Tennyson	King's	83	
Lent	G Hoffman	Caius	90	Last comp at Coldham Common

2. The CUGC captains and other officers, 1869-1914

As explained in Chapter 2, the initially founded Cambridge University Golf Club of 1869-71 had two recognised officers – George Gosset was the captain and Claude Carnegie was the honorary secretary. Andrew Graham Murray (subsequently Lord Dunedin) was clearly also a key figure but he is not recorded as holding a formal position.

The first recognised officers of CUGC during the Linskill era, beginning in March 1876 were Reverend George Pirie (captain), A H Evans (secretary) and W T Linskill (treasurer). Thereafter, until 1902-03, the captain, hon sec and hon treasurer were elected on a term-by-term basis, allowing for the possibility that there could be three holders of each post within each academic year.

One by-product of the research behind this book is a comprehensive listing of those who have held office since the club first existed. The Cambridge University Golf Club captains' board which hangs in the clubhouse of the Royal Worlington and Newmarket golf club commences with H (Harry) S Colt in 1889. If required, this can now be back-filled to 1869.

	Captain	College	Hon Secretary	College	Hon Treasurer	College
1869-71	G Gosset	King's	C C Carnegie	Trinity	n.a.	
1871-75	Club in abeyance					
1875-76						
Michaelmas	Club in abeyance					
Lent	Rev G Pirie	Queens'	A H Evans	Clare	W T Linskill	n.a.
Easter	Rev G Pirie	Queens'	A H Evans	Clare	W T Linskill	n.a.
1876-77						
Michaelmas	W T Linskill	Jesus	A H Evans	Clare	A H Evans	Clare
Lent	W T Linskill	Jesus	A H Evans	Clare	G M Frean	Trinity
Easter	G M Frean	Trinity	H E Corbett	Trinity	A H Evans	Clare
1877-78						
Michaelmas	W T Linskill	Jesus	J Stewart	Trinity	P R Don	Trinity
Lent	W T Linskill	Jesus	J Stewart	Trinity	P R Don	Trinity
Easter	W T Linskill	Jesus	J Stewart	Trinity	P R Don	Trinity
1878-79						
Michaelmas	W T Linskill	Jesus	J Stewart	Trinity	P R Don	Trinity
Lent	W T Linskill	Jesus	F H Lehmann	Trinity	P R Don	Trinity
Easter	W T Linskill	Jesus	R C Priestley	Trinity	P R Don	Trinity
1879-80						
Michaelmas	W T Linskill	Jesus	R C Priestley	Trinity	P R Don	Trinity
Lent	W T Linskill	Jesus	R C Priestley	Trinity	P R Don	Trinity
Easter	W T Linskill	Jesus	R C Priestley	Trinity	P R Don	Trinity
1880-81						
Michaelmas	W T Linskill	Jesus	R C Faithfull	Trinity	P R Don	Trinity
Lent	W T Linskill	Jesus	F E Ainger	St John's	R C Faithfull	Trinity
Easter	W T Linskill	Jesus	F E Ainger	St John's	R C Faithfull	Trinity
1881-82						
Michaelmas	W T Linskill	Jesus	E B Lehmann	Trinity	R C Faithfull	Trinity
Lent	W T Linskill	Jesus	E B Lehmann	Trinity	J L Casson	Trinity
Easter	W T Linskill	Jesus	E Armitage	Trinity	J L Casson	Trinity
1882-83						
Michaelmas	W T Linskill	Jesus	E Armitage	Trinity	J D Duff	Trinity
Lent	W T Linskill	Jesus	E Armitage	Trinity	J D Duff	Trinity
Easter	W T Linskill	Jesus	W P Frean	Trinity	J D Duff	Trinity

	Captain	College	Hon Secretary	College	Hon Treasurer	College
1883-84						
Michaelmas	W T Linskill	Jesus	W P Frean	Trinity	L H Evans	Pembroke
Lent	E F Chance	Caius	G Sandeman	Caius	L H Evans	Pembroke
Easter	E Armitage	Trinity	C E Allan	Jesus	L H Evans	Pembroke
1884-85						
Michaelmas	E Armitage	Trinity	A Clark	Jesus	J C Wilson	Jesus
Lent	E Armitage	Trinity	A Clark	Jesus	J C Wilson	Jesus
Easter	E Armitage	Trinity	A Clark	Jesus	B A F Grieve	Trinity
1885-86						
Michaelmas	A Clark	Jesus	C W Firebrace	Trinity	L G B J Ford	King's
Lent	A Clark	Jesus	C W Firebrace	Trinity	L G B J Ford	King's
Easter	A Clark	Jesus	C W Firebrace	Trinity	L G B J Ford	King's
1886-87						
Michaelmas	H B Boyd	Trinity Hall	J Craigie	Caius	R H Adie	Trinity
Lent	H B Boyd	Trinity Hall	W T Linskill	n.a.	R H Adie	Trinity
Easter	H B Boyd	Trinity Hall	W T Linskill		R H Adie	Trinity
1887-88						
Michaelmas	C W Burn	Trinity	W T Linskill		R H Adie	Trinity
Lent	C W Burn	Trinity	W T Linskill		R H Adie	Trinity
Easter	C W Burn	Trinity	W T Linskill		R H Adie	Trinity
1888-89						
Michaelmas	C W Burn	Trinity	W T Linskill		R H Adie	Trinity
Lent	C W Burn	Trinity	W T Linskill		R H Adie	Trinity
Easter	C W Burn	Trinity	W T Linskill		R H Adie	Trinity
1889-90						
Michaelmas	H S Colt	Clare	W T Linskill		R H Adie	Trinity
Lent	H S Colt	Clare	W T Linskill		R H Adie	Trinity
Easter	C H Cancellor	Trinity Hall	W T Linskill		R H Adie	Trinity
1890-91						
Michaelmas	C H Cancellor	Trinity Hall	W T Linskill		R H Adie	Trinity
Lent	H M Braybrooke	Pembroke	W T Linskill		R H Adie	Trinity
Easter	A M Joshua	Trinity	W T Linskill		P W Everett	Trinity
1891-92						
Michaelmas	J L Low	Clare	W T Linskill		A M Joshua	Trinity
Lent	J L Low	Clare	W T Linskill		A M Joshua	Trinity
Easter	J L Low	Clare	W T Linskill		A M Joshua	Trinity

	Captain	College	Hon Secretary	College	Hon Treasurer	College
1892-93						
Michaelmas	J L Low	Clare	W T Linskill		R C Burrows	n.a.
Lent	J L Low	Clare	W T Linskill		R C Burrows	
Easter	J L Low	Clare	W T Linskill		R C Burrows	
1893-94						
Michaelmas	A M Chance	Trinity	W T Linskill		R C Burrows	
Lent	A M Chance	Trinity	W T Linskill		R C Burrows	
Easter	A M Chance	Trinity	W T Linskill		R C Burrows	
1894-95						
Michaelmas	F R Upcher	Trinity Hall	W T Linskill		R C Burrows	
Lent	F R Upcher	Trinity Hall	W T Linskill		R C Burrows	
Easter	F R Upcher	Trinity Hall	W T Linskill		R C Burrows	
1895-96						
Michaelmas	K McL Marshall	Trinity	W T Linskill		R C Burrows	
Lent	K McL Marshall	Trinity	W T Linskill		R C Burrows	
Easter	K McL Marshall	Trinity	W T Linskill		R C Burrows	
1896-97						
Michaelmas	B Darwin	Trinity	C Pigg	n.a.	R C Burrows	
Lent	B Darwin	Trinity	C Pigg		R C Burrows	
Easter	B Darwin	Trinity	C Pigg		R C Burrows	
1897-98						
Michaelmas	P W Leathart	Clare	C Pigg		R C Burrows	
Lent	P W Leathart	Clare	C Pigg		R C Burrows	
Easter	P W Leathart	Clare	C Pigg		R C Burrows	
1898-99						
Michaelmas	A C Lawrence	Trinity Hall	C Pigg		R C Burrows	
Lent	A C Lawrence	Trinity Hall	C Pigg		R C Burrows	
Easter	A C Lawrence	Trinity Hall	C Pigg		R C Burrows	
1899-1900						
Michaelmas	E E Apthorp	Queens'	C Pigg		R C Burrows	
Lent	E E Apthorp	Queens'	C Pigg		R C Burrows	
Easter	E E Apthorp	Queens'	C Pigg		R C Burrows	
1900-01						
Michaelmas	A F Dudgeon	Trinity	C Pigg		R C Burrows	
Lent	W G Howarth	King's	C Pigg		R C Burrows	
Easter	W G Howarth	King's	C Pigg		R C Burrows	

	Captain	College	Hon Secretary	College	Hon Treasurer	College
1901-02						
Year	E W Hill Thomson	Pembroke	C Pigg		R C Burrows	
1902-03						
Year	H F H Caldwell	Trinity	C Pigg		R C Burrows	
1903-04						
Year	H C McDonnell	Corpus	C Pigg		R C Burrows	
1904-05						
Year	G Hoffman	Caius	C Pigg		R C Burrows	
1905-06						
Year	R C Simpson	Trinity	C Pigg		R C Burrows	
1906-07						
Year	M T Allen	Trinity	C Pigg		R C Burrows	
1907-08						
Year	V C H Longstaffe	Trinity Hall	C Pigg		R C Burrows	
1908-09						
Year	H B Hammond Chambers	King's	C Pigg		R C Burrows	
1909-10						
Year	E S Ulyat	Trinity	C Pigg		R C Burrows	
1910-11						
Year	J F Ireland	Trinity	C Pigg		R C Burrows	
1911-12						
Year	F M M Carlisle	Pembroke	C Pigg		R C Burrows	
1912-13						
Year	C Gardiner Hill	Pembroke	C Pigg		R C Burrows	
1913-14						
Year	R G C Yerburgh	Magdalene	C Pigg		R C Burrows	
1914-1919						
War years	Club in abeyance					

3. The CUGC Presidents, 1879-2016

Separate from the position of captain, the role of President of CUGC was also created in the early years of the club. The first recording of this was on 18 March 1879, when S R James, Esq., BA was noted to have been elected (the first) President. There have been thirteen Presidents to date. A brief biography of each President is provided below (with their years in office in parenthesis).

Sydney Rhodes James (1879) was admitted to Trinity in 1874. He obtained a BA (1st class) in Classics in 1878. He was a rugby Blue in 1876, 1877 and 1878 and captained Cambridge in 1877. He was ordained in 1883 and taught at Eton from 1879-97. From 1897-1914, he was Headmaster of Malvern. In the Great War, he served in the Royal Artillery Coastal Defence as Chaplain. After the War he returned to the church, rising to Archdeacon of Dudley. S R James only lasted one term as President, presumably due to leaving Cambridge to take up his position at Eton. He died in 1934, age 78.

James Edward Cowell Welldon (1879-1880) was reported to be the new President of CUGC on 18 Oct 1879 and held the role for one academic year. He had been admitted to Kings in 1873. He was a classics scholar, winning the Browne Medal in 1875 and the Chancellor's Medal in 1877 (both poetry prizes) and he was the Senior Classic (classics equivalent to Senior Wrangler in mathematics) in 1877. He was President of the Union in 1876. He was then a Fellow of King's from 1878-89. He was Head Master of Dulwich (1883-85) and Harrow (1885-98). Having been ordained in 1883 he served Queen Victoria as Chaplain (1888-98). He finished up as the Dean of Durham (1918-33) and died in 1937, age 83.

Reverend Augustus Austen Leigh (1880-1889) took on the role on 20 October 1880 and remained as CUGC President until May term 1889, a total of nine years. Austen Leigh was the sixth son of James Austen Leigh, the Vicar of Bray and the great nephew of Jane Austen. He came up to King's in 1859, yet another classics scholar (BA, 1863). He remained at King's thereafter as a fellow and ultimately became the Provost of King's (1889-1905). As well as being the President of the University Golf Club, he was also President of the University Cricket Club (1885) and the University Musical Society (1883-1905). He died in 1905, age 64.

Francis Darwin (1889-91), the third son of Charles, took over the role of President at the beginning of Michaelmas term 1889. Frank Darwin, as he was known, came up to Trinity in 1866 and took a BA in natural sciences (1st class). He worked with his father and, specialising in botany, he became a lecturer and reader at the University (1884-1904). After Charles Darwin's death in 1882, he also devoted himself to the organisation and publication of his father's life's work and letters. For his work, he was knighted in 1913. Francis was the father of Bernard Darwin who would go on to play golf for Cambridge and captain the club in 1896-97. He died in 1925, age 77.

Charles Pigg (1891-1896) was elected President of CUGC in October 1891. Charles Pigg was admitted to Peterhouse in 1875 taking his BA in 1879. He represented Cambridge in the Varsity golf match in 1886, being the only Cambridge man to win his match that year (Oxford winning 37 holes up). After graduating he had moved to Scotland to teach, which included ten years in St Andrews which no doubt included playing quite a bit of golf. He then returned to Cambridge where he worked for the next thirty years as a private tutor of students either seeking admission to the University or who required support in order to obtain their degree. He was also a good cricketer, playing for Northants (1874-75) and Herts. (1876-97). He died in 1929, age 72.

William Welsh (1896-1925) became the next President in October 1896. He had also represented Cambridge at golf in the Varsity match, playing in two of the early matches in 1880 and 1882 (there was no match in 1881 due to the weather). He won the Linskill Cup eight times, including six times in succession (when it was played for each term). William Welsh was born in Edinburgh in 1859. He was admitted to Jesus College in Michaelmas 1879 and obtained a BA in mathematics (Senior Wrangler) in 1882 and won the Smith's Prize for mathematics in 1883. In 1884 he became a fellow of Jesus and was a tutor from 1895 to 1919. He had been President for twenty-nine years and was closely associated with CUGC for forty-six years. The Welsh Cup was donated by past members of CUGC to commemorate him (see Appendix 4). He died in September 1925, age 66, while playing golf at Brancaster.

Sir Frank Ezra Adcock (1926-1966) became the next President following Walsh's death. Adcock had been on the CUGC Committee since the early 1920s. He may have become the President from October 1925 following Welsh's death in September. However, there are no minutes written up in the CUGC Minute

Book for 1925/26. He is definitely named as President for the year 1926/27. Frank Adcock was born in Leicester in 1886. He went up to King's in 1905 to study classics. He won several major prizes and obtained a double first. After some time spent in Germany, he became a fellow of King's in 1911 and a lecturer in classics. Apart from the war years, he spent his entire life in Cambridge thereafter, becoming the Professor of Ancient History in 1925, around the same time as he became President of CUGC. During both the First and Second World Wars he was involved in cryptography. During the First World War he was recruited into the so-called Room 40, the intelligence division of the Admiralty. He was awarded an OBE for his work there. In the Second World War he was at Bletchley Park and was responsible for the recruitment of a young mathematician from King's, Alan Turing. He was knighted in 1954, a few years after he had retired from the Chair of Ancient History. He held the position of President of CUGC until December 1966, a period of forty years. He died in 1968, age 82.

Sir Gordon Sutherland (1967-1980) became President from 1 January 1967. He was the Master of Emmanuel College at that time. Sutherland was born in Caithness in 1907 and graduated from St Andrews with degrees in physics and mathematics in 1929. He then spent two years in Cambridge and a similar period in Michigan doing experimental work on infrared spectrometry. During the First World War he was in Cambridge leading research on fuel analysis using spectrometry. After more time spent in Michigan he returned to the UK to head up the National Physical Laboratory from 1956-64. He was knighted in 1960 and was Master of Emmanuel from 1964-77. Sir Gordon remained as the President of CUGC until 25 April 1980, holding the position for thirteen years. He donated the Sutherland Cup (see Appendix 4). He died two months later in June 1980, age 73.

Dr Denis Marrian (1980-1993) became the ninth President in April 1980. Born in Yorkshire in 1920 and raised in Scotland, Denis Marrian graduated in organic chemistry at Manchester University. He moved to Cambridge in 1944 under Alex Todd who would win the Nobel Prize for Chemistry in 1957. In 1959 he became a teaching fellow at Trinity where he would subsequently become Senior Tutor and latterly fulfil the role of Praelector. He was a longstanding member of the Gog Magog Golf Club and played on Sundays in a group known as the 'Rutherford Four' (Lord Rutherford was one of the original founders of the fourball). In 1971 he was awarded the CVO (Commander of the Victorian Order) for his services to the Royal Family. He was Prince Charles's tutor at Trinity. He donated the Don's Cup (see Appendix 4). He died in 2007, age 86.

Professor Michael Powell (1993-1998) became President from June 1993 to October 1998. Mike Powell, who was born in London in 1936, was a mathematician who specialised in numerical analysis. After graduating from Peterhouse in 1959, he spent seventeen years at the Atomic Energy Research Establishment where he started the famous Harwell Subroutine Library. He returned to Cambridge in 1976 and was subsequently elected a Professorial Fellow at Pembroke holding the Chair of Applied Numerical Analysis. He was Captain of the Gog Magog Golf Club in 2005. He died in 2015, age 79.

Professor Haroon Ahmed (1998-2000) was President from October 1998 to June 2000. He was born in India in 1936, emigrated to Pakistan in 1947 and then took to the UK in 1954. He graduated from Imperial College, London and took his PhD at Cambridge. Haroon Ahmed is a scientist in the fields of microelectronics and electrical engineering and was Professor of Microelectronics at the Cavendish Laboratory from 1983-2003. He was elected a Fellow of Corpus Christi in 1967 and became the Master of the College from 2000 to 2006 and is now an Honorary Fellow. He still plays at the Gog Magog Golf Club.

Sir Roger Tomkys (2000-2010) was the President for ten years. He was born in 1937, was educated at Bradford Grammar School and graduated with a First in Classics from Balliol College, Oxford in 1960. Roger Tomkys spent his career in the diplomatic corps mostly in the Middle East. He was the High Commissioner in Nairobi from 1990-92 and was appointed KCMG in 1991. Upon retirement form the diplomatic service, Sir Roger served as Master of Pembroke College from 1992-2004 and chaired the Arab British Chamber of Commerce from 2004-10. He still plays golf at Royal Worlington and Newmarket Golf Club.

Professor Adrian Dixon (2010-) is the current President of CUGC, the thirteenth since records began in 1879. Adrian Dixon was born in Cambridge in 1948. He graduate from King's in 1969 and after initially pursuing a career in general medicine, he then specialised in radiology in which he has spent his entire career. He became a lecturer in radiology at Cambridge in 1979 and subsequently became the Professor of Radiology in 1994. He became a Fellow of Peterhouse in 1986 and was the Master of the College from 2008 to 2016. He is a member of the Gog Magog Golf Club, the Berkshire Golf Club, Royal Worlington and Newmarket Golf Club (Honorary) and a life member of Dooks Golf Club (Ireland).

4. The CUGC trophies, 1876-2016

Since it was established in 1878, the climax of the CUGC golfing year has been the annual Varsity match against Oxford University Golf Club. In support of this, over the years, CUGC (and OUGC) developed fixture lists against the major golf clubs in England to test their mettle and to provide guidance to the captain in the selection of his team in advance of the Varsity match. An additional element of preparation were the competitions held within the club. Over the years, since the earliest days, a number of cups and medals have been presented to the club to be competed for in a variety of formats. Most of these trophies are no longer played for and, in particular, a number of the earlier ones which were extensively reported on are no longer in the hands of the club. This appendix lists all of the CUGC trophies that have been identified together with some background about each of them and their whereabouts, if known.

They are listed in chronological order from when they were donated or first played for.

The Pirie Medal (1876)

The Pirie Medal, initially called the Terminal Challenge Medal, was presented by Rev George Pirie, the first Captain of the Linskill-inspired club formed in 1876. All we know about the medal is that it was silver.

It was first played for as a handicap prize in the first competition held at Coldham Common on 22 March 1876 and was won by Alexander Doleman. On the second occasion it was played for in November 1876, it was won by Reverend Pirie himself for the best scratch score. Thereafter it became the terminal prize for the best handicap-based net score.

This continued until November 1893 when its use was 'abolished'. Its place was taken by the Pirie Memento, a memento to be kept by the winner on each occasion it was played for. The Pirie Mementoes went to the best net score amongst players with handicaps of 16 and over. The Mementoes were provided by Munsey & Co, the silversmiths and jeweller in Cambridge. Nothing more is said in the club's minutes after November 1893 about the original Pirie Medal so it is not known where it might be.

Following the abandonment of Coldham Common, the Pirie Mementoes were played for at Whitwell Hill until the commencement of the First World War. After the war, it was minuted in February 1922 that the Linskill Cup and Pirie Memento were played for at the Gog Magog GC but that there were no sign of the cup or memento, 'all trace of them having been lost during the war'. The stock of mementoes was either lost or had run out. In any case that was the last occasion for which it was played. W H Aiken won with a net 75.

The Linskill Cup (1877)

The story of the search for and recovery of the Linskill Cup is told in detail in Chapter 10.

The St Andrews Medal (1889)

It was proposed by Mr R H Adie (Treasurer) in November 1889 that £3 be expended on a medal to be awarded, in a special handicap competition, in the Michaelmas and Lent terms and that a star be presented to each successive winner, and such medal to be called the Club Medal. The medal was described as:

> *Very handsome, and is made by Morris of King's Parade. On one side are the University arms and motto, and on the other St Andrew on the Cross. At the top are crossed clubs, bearing a scroll on which is inscribed "Far and Sure".*

This was first competed for on 11 March 1890. The first winner was E D Chetham Strode with a score of 105-18=87. This club medal was subsequently renamed the St Andrews Medal in December 1890. Initially it was played for on a different date from the terminal competition for the Linskill Cup and the Pirie Medal. However, in November 1893 it was decided to award the St Andrews Medal to the best net score in the terminal competition for players with handicaps less than 16 (while the Pirie Memento went to players with the best net score for 16 and over handicaps).

On 6 March 1908, the St Andrews Medal was played for and won by G H Greathead at Whitwell Hill with 85-9, net 76. This was the last occasion in which it is reported to have been played for. In the years following 1908 until 1914, when results were reported, it seemed that the Pirie Memento was open to all members as a handicap competition. This would infer that it had been decided to 'retire' the St Andrews Medal, maybe due to the declining number of members of the club. Alternatively, it went missing. Its whereabouts remains unknown.

The Barrow Medal (1892)

The Barrow Medal was donated by Claude L Barrow in 1892, an undergraduate member of CUGC at that time. It was originally played for in a bogey competition in the Michaelmas and Lent terms off two-thirds handicap. The interesting story of the Barrow Medal and its whereabouts is told in Chapter 6. It is made of silver gilt in the shape of a star with an enamel centre featuring the University of Cambridge coat of arms and the wording '*Non Sine Pulvere Palma* 1892'. On the reverse, there is the traditional golfing exhortation 'far and sure' and that it was won by I W Heron-Maxwell. As noted in Chapter 6, Heron-Maxwell was the second winner in November 1892 after H Parker had won when it was first played for in April 1892.

On 16 November 1909, the Barrow Medal was won by E J Hunter (Clare). No further reports or references to the Barrow Medal appear in either *The Cambridge Review* or the CUGC minute books. All we know thereafter is that the Barrow Medal was acquired at auction at Bonham's in June 2011 by an avid golf collector, Mr Jim McCormick from Chicago.

The Scratch (Gold) Medal (1910)

The Scratch (Gold) Medal was presented to CUGC by the Royal Worlington and Newmarket GC. The first winner in January 1910 was W E Gardner Beard with 79 at Worlington. It became colloquially known as the Trotter Scratch Medal after the Hon Secretary at Worlington, Mr W O Trotter who held the office from 1898-1923. In January 1936 it was recorded in the CUGC Minutes that at the request of the Secretary of Worlington, the Trotter Medal should in future be called the Worlington Medal. The medal was played for up until the Second World War. The last noted winners were: in 1939, J D A Langley, a Walker Cup player, with a score of 73; in 1942-43, D F Ashton; and in 1943-44, J R B Horden (Pembroke). Competition for the Scratch Medal was not revived after the war.

At the request of the author, a search for the Scratch Medal was carried out at Worlington. Thus far its whereabouts has not been discovered.

The Dunedin Cup (1928)

The story of the search for and recovery of the highly distinctive Dunedin Cup, encrusted with its seventeen half-crowns, is told in detail in Chapter 10.

The Welsh Cup (1929)

The Welsh Cup was first referred to in the club minutes in January 1929. It was purchased from donations raised by past members of CUGC in commemoration of William Welsh who was President of the club from 1892 until his death in 1925. It is recorded in the minutes in 1937 that Eustace Storey was one of the chief donors. It was originally played for in an inter-college competition. It is retained by the club today.

The Carr Challenge Cup (1930)

The Carr Cup was presented to the club by Sir William Emsley Carr in October 1930. Sir Emsley Carr was the proprietor of the *News of the World* as well as the editor of the paper from 1891-1941. Three of his sons, who all went to Trinity, represented Cambridge in the Varsity match: Walter Copley (nicknamed 'Wash') Carr (1928, 1929, 1930 and 1931), Harry (or Horace) Lascelles Carr (1931), who were identical twins, and William Emsley Carr (1933 and 1934). It was originally played for between eight players in a matchplay knockout format who had qualified via a bogey competition. The Carr Cup is retained by CUGC to this day.

The Dufferin Medal (1949)

Mention is made of the Dufferin Medal in the CUGC minutes on 9 May 1949 and also on one further occasion in 1950. It was not referred to thereafter and nothing more is known about it.

The Storey Medal (1952)

The Storey Medal was presented to CUGC by Eustace Storey in 1952. The medal had been awarded to him for being the runner-up in the Amateur Championship in 1924. He was the captain of CUGC in 1923-24. The Storey Medal was originally played for over 18 holes of medal play between the twelve players chosen to go to the university match (ten Blues plus the two reserves). It is retained by the club today.

The Ewen Cup (1959)

Ian Ewen (Pembroke 1933-36), who played in the Varsity match in 1936, offered to purchase and present a trophy to CUGC in January 1959. The committee decided that it should be played for over 18 holes under handicap as a bogey competition. Only two winners were ever recorded: 1961 – P R Johnston (Queens') 5 up; 1962 – T Piper (Pembroke) 3 up. It was not mentioned again in the CUGC minutes. Ian Ewen died at the age of 99 in Wellington, New Zealand in 2014. Correspondence with his daughter shed no light on the whereabouts of the Ewen Cup.

The Captain's Tankard (1972)

The Captain's Tankard was a tradition established by the captain of CUGC in 1972, Ian Pattinson. Mr Pattinson purchased a pewter tankard to be awarded to the player scoring the most points in CUGC matches in the run-up to the Varsity match. Subsequent captains also purchased tankards and this tradition was maintained for a number of years. (Since, the winners were able to keep the tankard that they had won, this is not strictly a CUGC trophy but has been included in this Appendix for completeness.)

The Sutherland Tassie (1973)

The Sutherland Tassie was presented by Sir Gordon Sutherland in 1973. He was President from 1967-80 (although on the actual trophy it says 1965-80). It was originally a scratch medal played for over 18 holes. The first winner was A D Burton (Jesus) with a score of 75. The Sutherland Tassie is retained by the club today.

The Don's Cup (1986)

The Don's Cup was presented to the club in November 1986 by Dr Denis Marrian who was President from 1980-93. The cup commemorates Sir Robert Speed. R W A Speed (Trinity) played for Cambridge in the Varsity matches in 1926 and 1927. In 1980, together with Sir Clement Penruddock (who represented Oxford in the same two Varsity matches), he founded the Speed Charitable Trust to provide financial assistance for golf at Oxford and Cambridge. The Don's Cup has been played in a variety of formats over the years involving golfing dons and the student members of the club and is retained by CUGC to this day.

In summary

If the Captain's Tankard is excluded, there are thirteen known historic CUGC cups and medals listed above. Of these, the club retained five in 2015: the Welsh Cup, the Carr Cup, the Storey Medal, the Sutherland Tassie and the Don's Cup. As a result of investigations while researching this book, the Linskill Cup and the Dunedin Cup were returned to CUGC in 2016. The Barrow Medal is held in private hands having been purchased at auction in 2011. The whereabouts of the remaining five – the Pirie Medal, the St Andrews Medal, the Scratch Gold Medal, the Dufferin Medal and the Ewen Cup – are unknown. Maybe a reader's memory will be jogged and the ones which still exist might be traced and in due course returned to CUGC.

Picture acknowledgements

Every effort has been made to locate and credit copyright holders of material reproduced in this book; the author apologises for any omissions. The author is grateful for permission for the use of materials provided to him.

Front cover, p53, Reproduced by kind permission of the Syndics of Cambridge University Library (the cover image is an amended version of Maps.BB.53.88.1); Back cover, p76, Courtesy of the Oxford & Cambridge Golfing Society and Rye GC; p5, p8, With kind permission of Christopher Hehmeyer; p15, p18, p31, p32, Ordnance Survey © Crown copyright; p23, North Tyneside Council; p25, By kind permission of the Royal and Ancient Golf Club of St Andrews; p29, Cambridgeshire Records Society; p43, Cambridge University Library, Microfilm.p467 vol 63; p61, By permission of the Master and Fellows of St John's College, Cambridge; p63, p95, p120, p122, p123, Courtesy of the University of St Andrews Library, ms38075, ms38075, ms38077, ms38075, ms38077; p66, Courtesy of Jim McCormick; p70, Cambridgeshire Collection, Central Library; p72, © National Portrait Gallery, London, artist George Charles Beresford; p80, © The GeoInformation Group, 2016; p87, From *Thomas Hodge, The Golf Artist of St Andrews*, Harry Langton, 2000; p124, Creative Commons Wikisource; p127, Historic Environment Scotland; p128, © 2016 Google; p131, Courtesy of Notts GC p138, By permission of the Master and Fellows of Pembroke College, Cambridge; p141, Charlotte Morrison; p142, By Leslie Ward 'Spy' for *Vanity Fair*, 1896; p146, Sunningdale GC

All other images are the property of the author.

Published by Michael B Morrison

© Michael B Morrison, 2016

ISBN 978-0-9956416-0-0

Design and production by Hart McLeod Ltd, Cambridge

Printed in England by Short Run Press Ltd, Exeter